Small Business Sales Dilemmas

50 Real Life Case Studies to Help you Sell More

Janet Efere

Copyright © 2017 Janet Efere

All rights reserved.

No part of this book may be reproduced or transmitted in any form or by any means, electrical or mechanical, including photocopying and recording, or by any information storage or retrieval system without permission in writing from the author.

Disclaimer

This book is written for informational purposes only. The author has made every effort to make sure the information is complete and accurate. All attempts have been made to verify the information at the time of publication and the author does not assume any responsibility for errors, omissions, or other interpretations of the subject matter.

The publisher and author shall have neither liability nor responsibility to any person or entity with respect to any loss or damage caused or alleged to be caused directly or indirectly by this book.

ISBN:
ISBN-13:

DEDICATION

This book is dedicated to all my lovely Tadpole Graduates who have been my constant inspiration

CONTENTS

1 - Think of a time when you had a really good buying experience. Why was it good?...1

2 - How will you ensure your prospective customer knows they can participate fully in the conversation? 3

3 - How and where will you position yourself in the customer's space when you visit them?...6

4 - After a customer says 'no' to your close, what strategies can you use to continue with the discussion? 9

5 - How are you going to get the attention of a prospect when you ring them for the first time? 12

6 - Have you ever talked yourself out of a sale and what should you have done differently? 15

7 - What can you do to establish rapport when you first meet a new customer?..17

8 - How will you ensure that all the important stakeholders are involved in the sale?..19

9 - How can you be sure that you are focusing on the correct customers? 22

10 - Are you making use of referrals to bring in business?......................24

11 - How can you encourage a potential customer to tell you about what is important to them?..26

12 - Are you embarrassed when you must sell?......................................28

13 - How can you ensure that you are selling using Benefits? 31

14 - How do you ensure you have a strong pipeline of potential customers? 34

15 - How can you ensure that you are communicating in a way that your customer can easily understand? 36

16 - What tools could you use to stop and refocus a sales call? 39

17 - How can you encourage yourself to sell when you feel demotivated?..42

18 - Sales funnels – are you using one of the simplest tools to sell more? 44

19 - How good are you at keeping customer records? 47

20 - Are you using the Power of Follow-up?..49

21 - Are you 'touching' your prospects enough?......................................51

22 - Are you looking after your existing customers well enough?..........53

23 - How can you upsell better? 56

24 - If you don't know your target, how will you know if you've achieved it? 58

25 - How can you ensure that you will gain your prospect's trust?........61

26 - When is a sale not a sale?..64

27 - How do you know if a customer is giving you buying signals? 66

28 - Do you have too many toxic customers?...69

29 - How well do you know your competitors? 72

30 - Are you selling ethically? 75

31 - Are you using the simplest and best tool to manage your time?....78

32 - Are you writing winning sales proposals? 81

33 - How can you overcome those days when you feel overwhelmed? 84

34 - Using customer feedback to sell more 87

35 - Are you leaving persuasive voice mails? 90

36 - Are you dressing right for your customers? 92

37 - What techniques can you use even if you are inexperienced at selling? 95

38 - Are you asking for the sale enough? 98

39 - How to make sure you are not using language that makes customers avoid you 101

40 - Do you proactively seek out your customers' pain points? 103

41 - Are you falling into the discounting trap? 106

42 - How can you keep sales strong at seasonally quiet times of the year? 109

43 - Are you making the most of the Competitive Advantage of being a small business? 112

44 - Are you trying to sell when you shouldn't be? 114

45 - Do your customers consider you a credible option? 117

46 - Can adversity help you sell more effectively? 120

47 - Are you prejudging your customers? 123

48 - Are you losing sales because you are not taking care of the little things? 125

49 - Are you trying too hard and offering too much? 128

50 - How do you know if you are getting 'out there' enough? 130

Preface

This book came about because I noticed that my students asked me about the same issues time and time again. I deal primarily with small businesses and entrepreneurs – people who are usually absolutely brilliant at what they do, but have often not had any formal sales or marketing training.

These amazing people launch their businesses with huge enthusiasm, work grindingly long hours and often make huge sacrifices. For some of them, the results come quickly, but for others it can take longer. Nearly every time, the reason is simple – they are just not selling enough. That can be for complex reasons, but often it is because of a lack of knowledge and skills.

This book is a compendium of 50 of the most common dilemmas I find business owners struggle with. Each one is set out in the same format:

- The Dilemma
- An explanation
- 5 Quick tips to help with the dilemma
- Case Study

Most of the case studies are based on my clients and their real-life situations (I have changed the names to protect the innocent!) but there are a few I adapted myself in order to cover some dilemmas I felt were essential.

The idea behind Small Business Sales Dilemmas is that you can use it in several ways. You can read it from cover to cover, you can dip into it as you need it, or you could choose one chapter per week and really focus on that area.

All I really want you to do is learn how to sell more and ensure your business thrives!

1 - Think of a time when you had a really good buying experience. Why was it good?

Although a lot of people think of a salesperson as someone to be avoided at all costs, the chances are that at some point you will, as the customer, have experienced great selling. If you can understand what makes the difference between an average and an outstanding sales experience, then you can use this knowledge to raise your own game and greatly improve your own success rate.

Knowledge is power and by making that little bit of effort to analyse and apply the techniques that sales masters use, your skills levels and confidence will increase, making the whole sales process much more enjoyable for both you and the customer.

Tips

1. **Take a genuine interest in your customers** Treat your customer as if they are the most important person in the world and give them your complete attention

2. **Ask lots of open questions to understand what is important to them** Open questions start with: what, when, why, where, how and who

3. **Listen more than you speak** There is an old adage that you have 'two ears and one mouth; use them in that proportion'.

4. **Make sure you know your product or service well** If you have a good knowledge of what you are selling, you will come across as credible, which helps to build trust.

5. **Use positive body language** Make sure you keep regular eye contact, smile and nod to show understanding and keep your posture open and welcoming. These non-verbal signals are particularly important while your customer is doing most of the talking

Case Study

In a class exercise, Suzanne was asked to remember when she bought something expensive and to explain why she bought it. Her example was when she bought a costly piece of jewellery for herself. In her discussion with the group, she revealed that she had wanted to buy an amethyst necklace but had been putting it off because she felt she couldn't justify the cost. However, on this occasion she had gone into a jewellery shop and met a salesperson who took the time to ask her about exactly what she wanted and why. He gave her his undivided attention, got various items out for her, some twice and nothing was too much trouble. He had a good knowledge of gemstones including amethysts and gave her some options she had not even thought of. When she finally decided on the piece she wanted, it required a small alteration, which he assured her could be done straight away. She ended up spending about 50% more than she planned, but she still has the necklace and it is still her favourite 12 years after buying it.

When probed, she admitted that the whole buying experience had been a pleasure for her – she had felt important because of the way the salesman had dealt with her, as the complete focus of his attention. He had gained her trust because of his knowledge, friendly manner and acknowledgement of what was important to her.

As the conversation developed, she had cared less and less about the price of the piece because she knew she was getting a special item which completely fulfilled all her requirements. In fact, she had become completely swept up in the whole process and realised that, within reason, she would have paid pretty much anything for that special piece of jewellery.

2 - How will you ensure your prospective customer knows they can participate fully in the conversation?

A sales meeting can be an unusual situation – who's in charge? Does one person have the advantage over another? What if there are several of you and only one customer?

There can be a lot of different dynamics in play, including variables such as the age and experience of the person you are meeting, their expectations of what you will be discussing, the amount of decision-making authority they have, the budget they have and whether they are trying to impress someone or are perhaps making a decision based on their career prospects. If they are nervous, then they may need guidance, whereas if they are (for example) an experienced buyer, they may just expect to sit back and let you pitch to them.

However, if you do not get participation from your customer, you stand very little chance of understanding what their needs and objectives are. Without this information, it will be very hard to make a sale.

Tips

1. **Have a written agenda.** It doesn't have to be complicated, but a simple agenda will immediately bring clarity to the meeting

2. **Gain verbal agreement to proceed.** Go through the agenda and ask them if they agree with what you have suggested. Say something simple like 'is that OK?'

3. **Add anything that is important to the customer.** So, for example if they want to discuss the intricate details of your latest widget, then add it to the agenda.

4. **Always allocate time to ask questions.** This might be at the end of the meeting, or all the way through, but emphasise that you want

to hear their questions.

5. **No matter how trivial-sounding the question may be, treat it seriously.** Most customers are far too busy to waste their time, so don't be suspicious of that strange sounding question – it could be something crucial.

Case Study

Marlon was an enthusiastic and energetic young entrepreneur and his business was starting to take off. He tried to visit at least two new potential customers every day to grow his customer base.

He had an appointment with the MD of a small manufacturing company – potentially a good new customer.

Such was Marlon's excitement that, at the beginning of the meeting, he launched straight into his planned sales pitch, hurriedly explaining how his company could help the MD in his search for greater efficiency. He had samples, case studies, testimonials and an excellent knowledge of his product. However, after about three minutes the MD held up his hand and said 'Stop!'.

Rather taken aback, Marlon paused. The MD quietly asked him 'son, what exactly do you want from this meeting?'. Marlon hesitated before answering 'I want to do business with you, sir.'

The MD nodded. 'And what do you think I want?' He gazed at Marlon who was now blushing. 'Er, I'm not sure sir, but I will try to find out'.

'Well that's a good start. Come back in one week and try again. Oh, and here are the contact details of Mr Dearn, my Facilities Manager – you will see him next time you come. Good day to you.'

Marlon left the office feeling completely bemused. What had just happened?

When he got back to his office, he called Mr Dearn to reschedule his appointment. Still confused, Marlon risked asking a question. 'When I was with your MD he stopped me talking and told me to reschedule with you. What did I do wrong?'

'Marlon, did you agree what you would be discussing in the meeting beforehand?'

'Er… yes I think so…' Marlon wasn't that sure himself anymore!

'Or did you – and think carefully about this – did you start talking to him without making sure it was a two-way conversation?'

Slowly, Marlon began to realise what had happened. Mr Dearn explained that his MD was a very busy man and that by agreeing to see Marlon, he must have thought it was worth spending time with him. However, having a sales background himself, he was a stickler for professionally conducted meetings. It turned out he had a pet hate, and that was not being consulted about how the meeting was going to progress.

Mr Dearn told him that he was lucky to get another chance. 'Go away, have a rethink and when you come and see me, make sure we both get to input – not just you'.

After a period of reflection, Marlon realised that he had been so hopeful of his chances that he had probably been a bit overbearing and had tried to control the meeting. He had been a bit intimidated and, instead of following his normal procedure, he'd nervously started talking, and had, in the process, completely alienating the MD.

The following week, when he had his meeting with Mr Dearn, Marlon made sure he didn't repeat those mistakes. He even dropped a handwritten note to the MD apologising. Embarrassed though he was, he was sensible enough to realise that he'd just been taught a very valuable lesson and, eventually he did end up securing a much sought-after contract with that customer.

3 - How and where will you position yourself in the customer's space when you visit them?

A sales meeting is a formal business meeting so should, theoretically, take place in business-like surroundings. However, in real life, that is not always possible.

You may end up meeting with potential customers in formal conference rooms, canteens, workshops, coffee shops, reception areas and almost any environment you can think of. Whilst you are a visitor, it does make sense to have a strategy to get the most out of any scenario and there are some simple things you can do to enhance your chances of having a successful and productive meeting.

Tips

1. **First Impressions**. Enter confidently, energetically and with positive body language

2. **Wherever possible, try to be seated with your customer** – it makes for a more professional meeting

3. **Let them take the lead** (after all, you are the visitor) and wait for them to suggest the seating arrangements

4. **If they offer you a tour of the premises, accept** – apart from this being polite, you can learn a lot about the company

5. **Sitting at 90° seems to work well** – opposite can be a bit confrontational, whereas next to them can be a bit uncomfortable

Small Business Sales Dilemmas

Case Study

Gemma was a business development executive in the food supplies industry and was in the process of trying to win a new account with a large wholesaler.

She had worked hard to get an appointment and had prepared well. However, when she arrived at her initial appointment with the customer, she was ushered through into a hectic purchasing department. There were no meeting rooms available and her contact asked if they could talk in the main office. He apologised for the noise but explained that they were under pressure because it was a busy time of year.

He sat at his desk, but there was no chair available for Gemma and she chose to stand. Although her contact was clearly keen to talk to her, he kept glancing at his computer and interrupted her several times to answer the phone. At one point, he even left to sort out an urgent despatch query. He apologised on his return and tried to give Gemma his full attention. They finished the meeting with a follow-up appointment booked in a week's time.

Gemma wasn't happy with the quality of the call. She had felt at a complete disadvantage by being forced to stand and was convinced she hadn't received sufficient attention from the customer, even though he had clearly been committed to seeing her.

At the next call, Gemma did several things differently. The day before the meeting, she rang the customer and asked if it would be possible to go somewhere quiet for their next meeting; if necessary perhaps leave the workspace and meet at a café. He couldn't do that, but he suggested the staff canteen might be suitable. He did, however, warn her that he would probably only be able to be out of the office for about 20 minutes.

When Gemma arrived, her contact had all his notes ready and took her through to the canteen. Sure enough, it was nice and quiet. He offered her a coffee and suggested a table near the production area. Gemma made sure she sat close enough to be able to show him information, but not so close that it was uncomfortable.

There were no interruptions at all and the meeting was very successful. As they were close to the production area, Gemma could ask lots of relevant questions about what she could see through the window. When they had finished the meeting, her contact asked her if she would like a tour of production, which she was only too happy to accept. Even though he had only committed to 20 minutes with her, they ended up spending nearly an hour and a half together.

Visiting the production area was very revealing and her contact chatted freely about new processes and products. As a result, Gemma picked up on a couple of key bits of information, which she later used in her proposal, which ultimately helped her to win the deal..

4 - After a customer says 'no' to your close, what strategies can you use to continue with the discussion?

When you are with a customer and you are trying to close a sale, at some point you will inevitably experience someone saying 'no' to you. They don't want it, they are not interested, they don't have the money, or a host of other reasons.

How you respond to this is important. Whether or not you have a sales background, you need to close sales in a business to make money, so how do you know when an objection is genuine and when it is not and whether you should try a bit harder?

Tips

1. **Try not to think of a 'no' as a 'no'** Instead think of it as 'I haven't had enough information to convince me to say 'yes' yet.'

2. **Rehearse what might happen** Practice in your mind (or out loud) what reasons the customer might give for saying 'no' and rehearse how you will respond, and you will be prepared if it happens.

3. **Mentally set yourself a target** For example, you might set yourself a challenge not to give up until the customer has said 'no' five times. Then, instead of being intimidated by the first rejection, you just feel like you've got it out of the way.

4. **Remind them what you can do for them** Repeat to the customer their goals or problems and state how the benefits of what you offer either help them achieve their goal or solve their problems.

5. **Don't sell it to them – get them to buy it from you!** People hate being sold to but they love to buy, so help them to imagine they already have your product or service. Ask them how it would feel if it was doing all the things it should and what it would mean to

them.

Case Study

Paul had been in office supplies sales for about six months and, although he was still inexperienced, he tried hard and was starting to do quite well.

One day, his boss gave him a lead – a customer wanted several thousand reams of paper each week. All Paul had to do was go in and 'ask' for the order – his boss explained that he had already done the work for him. 'Easiest sale you'll make all year" were his parting words.

Paul arrived feeling confident and quite excited and asked for the manager Mr Wenton. He duly came down to reception and invited Paul into his office. He was a friendly, outgoing man and was soon entertaining Paul with stories of how he had grown the business from one computer at home into a multi-million-pound company. Although Mr Wenton was extremely good company, Paul could hear his manager's words ringing in his ears and, as soon as he had the chance, he decided to ask for the order – after all, he had been there for over 30 minutes and he had hardly got a word in edgeways. His manager was going to be wondering what was happening.

"Mr Wenton" began Paul, "I really came here because my manager said you wanted to order 3,000 reams of paper each week. Shall we do the paperwork, so that I can get back to the office with it?"

Mr Wenton paused. Then he told Paul that he hadn't made his mind up yet. That completely took the wind out of Paul's sails. He had not expected that! He had expected a cheerful 'yes'. What would his manager say?

He tried one more time: "But my manager said it had all been arranged"

That didn't work either. Paul left the office disconsolate, dreading the forthcoming conversation with his manager.

Although his manager was not happy with Paul, he could tell it was inexperience that had caused the problems. He went through the call with Paul. Had he built rapport and shown interest in Mr Wenton and his business - no not really. Had he taken the trouble to find out why Mr Wenton wanted the paper and why he had chosen them to supply it - again, no. Finally, had Paul checked that there was nothing else worrying Mr

Wenton, or any details he wanted clarifying to give him reassurance - no.

Armed with this information, Paul reluctantly made another appointment to see Mr Wenton. He apologised for trying to rush him into deciding and went through everything his manager suggested. To his surprise, a beaming Mr Wenton agreed to place a weekly trial order of 3,000 reams for the next three months and to review the situation after that time. Paul had learned a very valuable lesson.

5 - How are you going to get the attention of a prospect when you ring them for the first time?

It can be very hard to gain the attention of someone on the phone. People are busy, there are lots of distractions and as soon as they think you are going to try and sell them something, the normal reaction is to try and get rid of you as quickly as possible. However, it is a fact that a lot of business is done by contacting people by telephone, so it is a valuable tool for a salesperson to use. There are also ways of getting and keeping your prospect's attention, which of course, improves your chance of ultimately getting a sale too.

Tips

1. **Don't be apologetic**. You have a genuine reason for calling, so why should you apologise?

2. **Don't ask 'how are you today?'** It screams 'I'm trying to sell you something' and your prospect will immediately switch off

3. **Get to the point quickly.** Don't ramble – people are busy and if you waste their time, they will get rid of you

4. **Ask for help.** Most people are decent human beings and will try to help you if you explain what you want in a pleasant way

5. **Speak clearly.** If they can't understand what you are saying, then they won't be interested in talking to you

Case Study

Juliet was a new sales manager. Her small team were performing well, but she had noticed that most of the sales were repeat business. Juliet knew that the team also needed to focus on bringing in new customers to maintain and improve on performance.

She set the team a task to identify the best ways of contacting people on the phone, based on their experience within their market. It was immediately apparent that most of the team hated cold calling and would do pretty much anything to avoid it!

Undeterred, Juliet scheduled in some training and, encouraging the high performers to share best practice, identified some key strategies to help them when ringing customers for the first time.

Over the next few months, they reviewed what they had learned and were able to discuss what worked the best. They found:

1. There is no such thing as a standard approach – individuality often works better, as people will only really buy from people they like
2. Preparation is vital before a phone call – always make sure you know who you are ringing and whether they are the right contact. Make sure you know how to pronounce their name.
3. Have objectives for the call – not every call is going to result in a meeting or a sale, but if you know what you are trying to achieve you are more likely to achieve it
4. Plan what questions you are going to ask beforehand
5. Anticipate objections and prepare how best to deal with them
6. Be nice to gatekeepers – they can both block you and provide lots of information
7. Although it is OK to use notes, don't use a script – it is obvious to the person on the phone that you are using one, because you don't sound natural
8. Work out exactly what you are going to say to start with and practice it repeatedly – you will only have a few seconds to get their attention so be clear, relevant and professional.
9. The more calls you make, the better you will get, so even if you don't feel like it, keep trying, keep learning and keep trying to improve
10. There were very clear benefits to using the company's products and if the salespeople could mention at least two benefits in the initial call, they were much more likely to get an appointment.
11. Make sure you always have a diary available to book appointments – having done the hard work and gained agreement to a meeting, you don't want to risk it by not being organised

Although no one in the team said they had suddenly started enjoying cold calling, there was much less resistance to it and new business was tangibly rising after the team's training.

6 - Have you ever talked yourself out of a sale and what should you have done differently?

It is important to understand when to talk and when to stop. When we are being sold 'to' none of us likes to be with someone who talks constantly; it is irritating and it can make us feel resentful because it is taking up our time. This is especially true if we have already made our mind up to buy.

When you are the one doing the selling, you should also be aware that not every customer needs to know everything about your product or service – all they really need to know is whether it will solve their problem or meet their objective and how. Anything else is just clutter and can put the sale at risk.

Tips

1. **Once the customer has confirmed they want to buy, then stop talking and deal with the practicalities** In other words, sort out the payments, the order form, the invoice or whatever, and conclude the transaction.

2. **Don't try and fill the silence** It is human nature to try and fill uncomfortable silences with words, especially if you are nervous. Resist the urge.

3. **People buy from people they like and trust.** If you start to become irritating through talking too much, they may still walk away because they can't bear the thought of having to deal with you again.

4. **Write it down**. If you are prone to nervous chatter, write a checklist of things you can do to conclude the deal. That will keep you on the straight and narrow and stop you waffling.

5. **When you are buying something, observe what other people do when they sell to you.** Once the sale has been agreed, what do

they do or say and is it something you could do too?

Case Study

Michael ran a photography business and believed passionately in what he did. He was versatile and could do portrait and architectural photography so had a good base of potential clients. However, because he was foremost an artist, he struggled with the business transaction side of his work, much preferring to discuss techniques, composition, lighting and colour.

When a potential client was interested in engaging him, he would talk passionately and with knowledge about what was required, taking trouble to understand the requirements of the project. Although he never seemed to directly ask for the work, he often got jobs because he was so clearly a good fit and because people loved his enthusiasm.

One day he did just this – he met a potential client, who liked him and the project was his!

Michael should have concluded the deal, shaken hands and arranged the start of the job right then. Instead, because he couldn't quite believe his luck, Michael continued to talk about photographs, previous clients, his working techniques and anything he could think of. It was during this nervous chatter, that he revealed a previous job he had worked on. His new client was familiar with it (he was in the same industry) and it turned out that he didn't think much of the final pictures. To make matters worse, he knew the person who had overseen the project and had heard from her that the photographer had been difficult to work with – rather too fussy and had taken a long time to set up the shots.

The new client quietly made his excuses and left. Michael never heard from him again.

7 - What can you do to establish rapport when you first meet a new customer?

There are all sorts of reasons why it can be difficult when you first meet a prospective customer. Whether they are visiting you in your shop or you have made an appointment to see them, you can't dive straight in and start selling – there are certain 'norms' you must negotiate.

So much of good selling relies on relationship building, so it makes sense to get the first bit right. In a first meeting, you will tend to start with certain accepted protocols – the meeting and greeting part forms the foundation of the entire business relationship, so you want to get off to a good start.

Tips

1. **Smile and say 'hello'!**

2. **Shake hands** – it is the accepted way to start a business meeting

3. **Use small talk** – the weather, the traffic – anything simple and uncontroversial

4. Keep your **body language** open and friendly

5. **Be yourself** – don't try and pretend you are someone you are not – people can spot when they are dealing with someone who is insincere

Case Study

As a new sales representative, Claire was determined to prove herself in her role. She was conscientious about making appointments but didn't seem to be making sales. Feeling the pressure, she asked her manager for advice and he agreed to accompany her on a sales call.

They had an appointment with Mike, a high-level contact from a software company. Claire introduced her manager and he and the contact chatted trivialities such as the terrible traffic and the effect the cold weather was having on the rush hour drive. Claire didn't say anything. She was impatient to get on with the meeting.

They sat down to begin their formal discussion and Claire efficiently and professionally started the meeting, correctly asking questions about the business. After a couple of minutes, her manager interrupted and said 'sorry to interrupt Claire, but I would really like to know a little bit more about what makes Mike tick and what he is trying to achieve here. Would you mind if we did that first?'

Her manager then proceeded to chat to Mike as though they were old friends. They discovered his hobbies, why he loved his job, what he was trying to achieve and some of the things that caused him problems and annoyed him. Then her manager asked Claire to resume from where she stopped and they all started to talk about specific business issues that were relevant to both companies. Seamlessly, the conversation went through some possible solutions which Claire's company could provide and they walked out of the meeting with an order.

Claire's manager explained to Claire that being efficient and professional wasn't enough on its own. 'People buy from People. In other words, show them that you're a human being first and a company representative second.' He gave her the instruction that at every future meeting, she was to make sure she smiled a bit more, ask a couple of ice-breaking questions and try and find out about what the prospects liked doing when they weren't at work. Armed with her new tools, Claire's closing rates immediately started to improve and she realised that spending a couple of minutes on relationship building at the beginning of the call made an enormous difference to her effectiveness.

8 - How will you ensure that all the important stakeholders are involved in the sale?

In sales, you can easily waste a lot of time if you don't deal with all the people who are involved in the decision-making process. If your customer is a business, you may well end up having to negotiate through deciders, influencers, finance, end users and initiators. They form something called a Decision-Making Unit (DMU), which is an informal 'team' of people who are all involved, but who often have different priorities and roles.

Even if you are just dealing with one customer, then you may well find that someone else is paying, or will have influence.

A useful Acronym to help you is MAN, which stands for MONEY, AUTHORITY, NEED. In other words, you should always try to deal with the MAN when you are selling.

Tips

1. **Always try to speak to the MAN**

2. **Be sensitive** Your contact might be passionate about your product or service but don't alienate him or her by asking questions like 'Who is really in charge?' Just because your contact is not necessarily the most senior person in the DMU, remember they could be the best ambassador for you. You want them to be on your side!

3. **Ask who needs to be involved** A simple question you can ask to find this out is: 'Who else is involved in the decision-making process?'

4. **Ask for a diagram** If you don't understand the decision-making process in a company, it can be helpful to get them to draw you a simple diagram to explain it.

5. **Everyone is important** When you have found out all the key contacts, remember to treat them all respectfully, regardless of status.

Case Study

Kevin was an experienced salesperson within the reprographics industry. He regularly achieved his target and was well respected. As the year ended, he was a front runner to be top salesperson in the country, with a prestigious holiday and bonus to be won if he achieved it.

He had one existing customer who he knew might be able to place a substantial order just before the year end. Whilst nothing was guaranteed, there was a good chance that, if this order was placed, Kevin would win his prize. Being a good salesman, he arranged for a visit to see this customer.

The customer had dealt with Kevin regularly over the years and knew he could provide good work on time and to the required standard. However, this would potentially be the biggest money value order he had ever placed with Kevin.

Before the meeting, Kevin prepared. He went through his notes, checked what the customer had liked and tried to work out if there were any weaknesses in his proposal. He made sure he had something he could use to reassure the customer for any potential objection.

At the meeting itself, Kevin tried to put his nerves to one side and concentrate on his customer's needs, as he had been trained to do. He didn't rush – instead, he took time to ask good open questions about the importance of the project and what the customer required of him. He summarised, checked, questioned and took care not to pressurise his customer.

When the customer raised some concerns, Kevin was ready with a testimonial which addressed the exact same issue. He knew all his figures and, although there was one thing he couldn't do for the customer, he was very open about it and had an alternative ready, which was acceptable to his customer.

There was one unexpected question about the specification of something rather technical. Kevin admitted he didn't know the answer, but made a phone call there and then to the production facility. They answered it simply and quickly which reassured the customer completely.

When Kevin asked for the order, the customer immediately said yes, happy that his project was in safe hands. When Kevin got back to the office and worked out the exact specification of the project, he was delighted to discover that it was an even bigger order than he had expected. He put the order through, confident that he should have done enough to win salesperson of the year.

9 - How can you be sure that you are focusing on the correct customers?

There is a well-known rule, known as the 'Pareto' rule, which applies to many industries, but in particular, sales. Very simply, this states that 80% of your sales come from 20% of your customers. Interestingly, there is an inverse rule too, which states that 20% of your customers cause 80% of your problems! So, from time to time, it is good practice to examine all your customers, assess how much business they bring you and how easy or difficult they are to deal with. It may be that you will need to do some pruning and get rid of the least productive 20% allowing you to focus on the most profitable and get more of the same.

Tips

1. **Remember** – busy is not the same as productive

2. **20% of your customers will generate about 80% of your business** – these are the ones to really look after

3. **80% of your customers will generate 20% of your business.** These are the ones to lose

4. **Don't go with 'feelings'** – check the figures to give you the bigger picture

5. **Once you know who the ideal top 20% of customers are,** you can seek out more like them

Case Study

Warren had just been employed as the new sales rep for a reprographics firm. He had inherited a decent number of customers and the first few weeks were a flurry of rushing around, collecting jobs, putting orders through the system and getting to know the ropes.

However, after a couple of months, he realised that despite the effort he was putting in, he was only just achieving his target and, whilst lots of his customers were spending, his whole time was taken up with account management and he was not developing the business by getting new accounts.

There was a good record system in place, so Warren sat down and decided to work out which customers were bringing in the most money. Out of the 76 who had spent money since he joined, he realised that 12 of them were ordering at least once a week and a further 5 had placed at least 3 orders.

He then looked at the ones who were spending the least. 5 of them hadn't spent much, but they also had not been any trouble either. However, what really jumped out at him was that there were 6 customers who were really time consuming – regularly asking for quotes, pickups, or just changing the spec. Once he factored in the cost of his time, he reckoned that it was costing the company money to service these accounts.

He showed his findings to his manager, who told him to do whatever he wanted, as long as he was bringing in more money. Although interestingly, when he saw some of the names, he said he didn't like doing work for those customers anyway because they always tried to cut them down on price.

Armed with this permission, Warren did two things.

Firstly, he set about making appointments with all his top customers to see if he could grow the accounts.

Secondly, he rang the 6 customers he had highlighted as difficult and informed them that there was going to be a significant price increase. He then went on to recommend an alternative reprographics provider who he felt might be better able to serve them. There was a bit of grumbling, but he stood his ground and said that whilst his company would be happy to quote, he felt he was unlikely to be competitive in the future.

It worked. No longer distracted and busy with his time-wasting customers, Warren could focus on his best customers and began to steadily grow the business, to everyone's satisfaction.

10 - Are you making use of referrals to bring in business?

Referrals can be one of the most effective and simplest ways to get new business. At the most basic level, a referral is when you ask someone to recommend your services to someone else, usually because you have delivered some sort of work to them. Although referrals can sometimes be rewarded financially (either formally through a referral scheme or informally), sometimes it is just enough to say a genuine 'thank you' to the person who recommended you.

Ways to get referrals:

1. **Offer a reward** – financial or other

2. **Give someone else a referral first** – people tend to want to reciprocate since 'one good turn deserves another'

3. **Ensure the service you give is so amazing that people will want to recommend it to others**

4. **Ask!**

5. **Be specific** about the type of people you want to be introduced to

Case Study

Susan opened an independent gym in a small bustling town just on the outer part of the main high street. She knew that it would take time to get going and she was hoping to get lots of local business as the next closest gym was 4 miles away.

One day, Susan's regular hairdresser announced she was moving to another part of the country. Susan needed to find a new one. As there was a professional looking salon just opposite her gym, she decided to try them out.

The salon was owned by Sandra, a bubbly, chatty and engaging young woman who seemed to know absolutely everyone in the town and was full of information about who to use for what and where to find it. As Susan talked with her, the beginnings of an idea began to form. She made a proposal to Sandra. In return for free gym membership with access to all the facilities, would Sandra be prepared to recommend clients to her? Sandra was delighted (she had been intending to join the new gym anyway as it was so close and now she was getting offered free membership!). As an extra, Susan would recommend her salon in return – she was delighted with her haircut, so knew she would probably have referred people there anyway.

If this arrangement worked, it should be a 'win win' for both businesswomen.

So, Sandra tried out the gym and loved it.

The referrals started coming thick and fast. It turned out that not only was Sandra chatty, she was very persuasive and nearly every day, Susan got another new enquiry. However, Susan was helping Sandra too. She had received a lot of compliments on her new hair style and was more than able to persuade people to try Sandra's Salon. She also noticed an interesting trend; a lot of her lady customers had both disposable income and time on their hands and often, they came to the gym, did their exercise and took a shower, but instead of going home to get ready, if Susan suggested it, they popped over to Sandra's Salon to get their hair done.

Sandra and Susan not only ended up growing both their businesses, but became firm friends as a result.

11 - How can you encourage a potential customer to tell you about what is important to them?

To sell to a customer, you need to understand what is important to them and what problems or objectives they have. By asking good questions and listening carefully to the answers, you will really start to understand what matters to them and later this will help you fit your product or service to their requirements. To get your prospect to 'open up', you should ask lots of open questions which encourage detailed answers. These are questions starting with: what, when, why, where, how and who.

Tips

1. **Ask 'open' questions** to get the customer to respond in detail.

2. **Don't interrupt them**, let them speak

3. **Remember the 2:1 rule** – you have 2 ears and one mouth, so use them in that proportion

4. **Use positive body language** to show you are interested in what they have to say

5. **Remember to take notes** – it shows you are taking a professional interest but it also means you will remember what was said.

Case Study

Dale ran a technical design company. He had a few regular clients but was trying to get some more. Although he was brilliant at what he did, he hated the selling side of things and wherever possible, avoided conversations with potential customers, preferring to leave that to one of his two colleagues.

However, one day an enquiry came in from the owner of a local business. They were interested in finding out more about his services. Dale took the phone call and the caller asked if Dale could come and meet them and get to know the buyer. Realising there was the chance of business, Dale reluctantly agreed.

He told his partner Tracy, who said she knew the buyer at the company and that he was a tough negotiator. Realising that Dale was probably out of his depth, she sat at her desk and wondered what she could do to help him. She could go to the meeting with him, but actually, he probably needed some more practical help.

The next day, she gave him a list of questions. She told him that he must ask all the questions during the meeting and write down whatever the buyer said. He read the list and, although he didn't necessarily see the importance of the questions (which seemed to have nothing to do with technical design) he took them with him. The questions were:

- What do you hope to get out of this meeting?
- What is important to you when you are choosing a trusted supplier?
- What is your process for managing your projects?
- Who are your ideal customers?
- How are you doing compared to your main competitors?
- Where are the main challenges within your business now?
- What are your future plans?
- What is the decision-making process in your organisation?
- What would it mean to you if we could help you overcome some of your challenges?

Armed with his list of questions, Dale went into his meeting with the buyer. About an hour later, Dale returned and came and sat next to Tracy. He explained that the buyer had initially been quite frosty and unforthcoming, but as Dale began asking him questions from the list, he had gradually opened up. In fact, he had become almost too talkative. By the time Dale got to the last question, the buyer had asked if Dale was free to start work on a new project in 2 weeks, and he hadn't even mentioned the price.

Dale successfully completed this project and continued to get further work. Later, the buyer confided in him that Dale had taken such an interest in him and what was important to him was that he felt Dale could be trusted.

12 - Are you embarrassed when you must sell?

How many times have you been approached by someone trying to sell something who seems uneasy, nervous, or just a bit shifty? Perhaps they are too self-deprecating or they criticise their own product or service. As you edge away from them, all you really want to do is get away – buying from someone like this is the last thing on your mind.

Many people don't like the thought of selling, but they know they need to sell, so they do it, but they feel embarrassed.

This embarrassment shows up through:

- Speech (too fast, wrong words, lots of umms and errrrs, apologising too much)
- Body language – feeling embarrassed = looking embarrassed (poor eye contact, wringing hands, shifting from foot to foot)
- Too quick to agree to discounts, extras or impossible deadlines, which impact on profitability

So why would you feel embarrassed? Well, typically people have a lot of preconceptions about sales people – they think they are pushy, won't stop talking, will persuade you to buy something you don't want, act charming to get you to like them, and might rip you off. Not exactly the most popular type of person, is it? Not someone you would want to be either. And herein lies much of the problem – most people want to be 'liked' and they perceive a salesperson as someone who won't be liked.

Tips

1. **Make a list** of all the good things your product or service can do
2. **Work out what you do better than your competitors**
3. **Ask satisfied customers for testimonials**
4. **Tell people what you do as a story** (it feels less 'salesy' and everyone loves a story)

5. **Practise saying all the above out loud** where no one can hear you – in the car is a good place

Case Study

Davina was bright, bubbly and loved her job as a children's party organiser. She knew everything there was to know about balloons, party tricks, children's songs and party games. Once engaged to organise a party, she could be trusted to manage everything smoothly and professionally and her business grew steadily as she got lots of repeat business.

However, when her husband's work meant that she had to move to a completely different part of the country, she began to struggle. Although she retained some customers, the nature of her work meant that most of her clients now lived too far away. She faced a stark choice: get more new business or close.

Even with her tremendous track record, Davina lacked confidence in her ability to sell. She had got used to receiving referrals, recommendations and repeat business, so the thought of selling to strangers suddenly seemed overwhelmingly difficult. She particularly struggled when she had to talk about the cost of her service – after all she really enjoyed what she did and felt guilty asking for money. As a result, the few deals she did secure were discounted and it soon became clear that she was only just breaking even.

Her husband realised she was in difficulty and suggested she get some help with her marketing. So, she took his advice and decided to get her website updated. Perhaps if her business had a bit of a fresh new feel, then the business might start to come.

She engaged a local web designer to help. The designer started to ask lots of questions about the business; what was unique about it, what made it special, why did people keep coming back again and again? As Davina opened up to her web designer, she began to realise that she had completely forgotten what made her business great. She quite surprised herself with how many wonderful things she had achieved and how many children and parents she had helped over the years. It was when the web designer asked to see the testimonials from happy customers that Davina really got it! She had a terrific business which had brought happiness to hundreds of children and peace of mind to their parents. Why was she embarrassed about that?

Re-energised and with a new website ready to go, Davina started contacting people with enthusiasm. She made sure she always had the website open in front of her to help her remember all the good things about her business. She used the testimonials from satisfied clients to inspire her when the going got tough. She even developed a good line in overcoming parents' objections regarding price – 'can you put a price on your child's happiness and your peace of mind?'

Whilst she didn't get it right all the time, Davina was able to use one of her most attractive assets – her engaging personality when speaking with customers. She learned to focus on how she brought happiness to children and their parents and completely forgot to be embarrassed! Once more, sales started to increase and repeat business began to build. She also learned to regularly re-read her testimonials as a reminder of why she was good at her business.

13 - How can you ensure that you are selling using Benefits?

When a salesperson just talks and talks, it is off-putting. It's as though they are trying to 'throw' as much information as possible at you in the hope that eventually they will get the one bit that is important to you. In the meantime, you have either fallen asleep, lost the will to live or just walked off.

To be effective when you are talking to a customer, you need to not just tell them the features of your product or service, but the benefits of it to them. That way, they understand exactly how it will help them.

Even if it sounds obvious, the customer might not realise what the benefits are for themselves, so smart sales people know to always taken the time to explain the benefits.

Tips

1. **A feature** is a physical quality of the product or service

2. **A benefit** is the way that this feature is useful

3. **If you can turn all your features into benefits**, it makes your product or service much more appealing

4. **Link a feature and a benefit by saying.** "A feature of this product is AAA and the benefit of this is BBB"

5. **Practice on something simple** like a cup or a chair and see if you can work out the features and benefits of each.

Case Study

Obi had just started his sales career as a sales assistant in a large retail outlet. He was working in the household department and was put under the supervision of Stan, the senior salesperson in the team.

Obi really wanted to prove himself and wasted no time in getting stuck in and helping customers wherever he could. Although he was doing well, he couldn't help but notice that Stan was way ahead of him in the figures, particularly on the higher value items. He decided to ask Stan for some help. Stan was more than happy to assist because he could see that Obi had potential.

Stan decided to teach Obi about the difference between features and benefits. He explained that a feature was a physical attribute of the item for sale and a benefit was the way that physical attribute was useful. He began with something simple – a pair of rubber gloves.

What were the features of the gloves? There were two main ones – they were made of strong rubber and had a special heatproof coating. So, what were the benefits? The strong rubber meant that they were less likely to split or break, so lasted longer. The heatproof coating meant that the person using them could do the washing up in hotter water without getting burned.

Obi understood the lesson, so they moved onto something else – a set of expensive crystal glasses. What were the features – well they were made of the finest glass, had exceptional clarity and were hand finished.

Stan encouraged Obi to work out the benefits. These expensive glasses were a status symbol. The owners could enjoy knowing that they had paid for something special, which most people couldn't afford. These glasses would enable the owners to showcase their purchase when serving fine wine and it would complement their expensive dinner service when they had visitors over for a dinner party. The glasses would not only last a lifetime, they could even be an heirloom for future generations. This time the benefits were a little less practical, but were nevertheless very important to people in the market for such items.

Stan encouraged Obi to start automatically looking for benefits in everything. So instead of just listing all the features (which meant the customer had to work out for themselves whether it was important) Obi was helping them to understand why the features were important.

Soon it became second nature to Obi to describe things in this way. He did start to sell more but he also noticed that customers spent more time with him too, because they felt that he understood them better. All in all, he found his job much more satisfying because he knew he was helping his customers make better buying decisions.

14 - How do you ensure you have a strong pipeline of potential customers?

It is important to have a pipeline of potential customers. This will be a mixture of enquiries, prospects, returning customers and leads – some 'hot' and some quite 'cold' that the person responsible for generating sales will manage. It is their job to move customers through the pipeline until they get to the stage where they are ready to buy. If you think of it a bit like a sausage machine, you need to keep putting new prospects and leads in the whole time at one end, to ensure that paying customers come out the other end. If you stop feeding it, then you stop getting sales!

Tips

1. **Have a system for managing your pipeline** – it can be a simple diagram or something generated by a special piece of software, but you must have something

2. **The more you put in, the more will come out the other end**, so keep topping it up regularly

3. **Pay attention to all your leads and prospects** – not just the big ones

4. **Do not be distracted by the thought of winning big** – there is more than one way to bring in business and lots of smaller accounts might be better than putting all your eggs in one basket

5. **Keep contacting all the people in your pipeline regularly** – some will fall out from time to time and by regular contact you will see how healthy your pipeline is and whether you need to add to it.

Case Study

Matt worked for a large photocopier company. He was responsible for selling mid-range machines and consistently hit his target.

When a large opportunity came up with a local authority, Matt discussed it with his manager and they agreed it was worth his while to pursue it as it would deliver nearly his entire annual target if he won it. Matt's manager did caution him not to neglect his other customers and to ensure he continued to prospect for new customers. Matt was more than happy to agree to this – he had calculated that, while the local authority deal was going to be time-consuming to win, he would have plenty of time to manage both his existing customers and develop new accounts.

Indeed, Matt could do this very effectively and, 2 months later, he had made good progress with all his work. However, by the third month, he failed to meet his target and thereafter each month his figures kept dropping as he needed more and more time to pursue the local authority account and he had less time to create new leads and move them through the pipeline.

When his manager expressed concern, Matt could reassure him that he was making really good progress with the local authority deal and, once it came in, then his figures would be way up again. In fact, they were talking about increasing their overall spend by about 20%.

On the day before the decision was due to be made, Matt received a telephone call from the local authority. Central Government had ordered that with immediate effect, all expenditure above a certain level was to be halted indefinitely. That meant Matt's deal would not now go ahead.

Matt couldn't believe it. He told his manager, who whilst sympathetic, was not happy. They sat down to analyse the situation – there was really nothing that could be done.

That then left the problem of Matt's poor sales figures – now there was no large deal coming in, his manager wanted to know what other projects were in the pipeline to bring him back over target. The truth soon became apparent – Matt had focussed nearly all his energy into winning this local authority account and had almost completely neglected his pipeline of enquiries and prospects. He had no new business scheduled for at least 2 months and only a handful of prospects.

Demotivated and exhausted, Matt had to pretty much start again from scratch. In the end, he found it so hard to claw his way back up to target that he finally decided to leave and get a job elsewhere.

15 - How can you ensure that you are communicating in a way that your customer can easily understand?

Just because you know what you are talking about, it doesn't necessarily mean that your customer will. Remember, they may be coming to you as an expert in your field.

Also, people can be reluctant to admit that they don't understand – no one wants to look stupid and often they would much rather say nothing and walk away, than ask for clarification. The trouble is, if that is a potential customer, they could be walking away from spending money with you.

Also bear in mind that people have different knowledge, abilities and can also experience genuine barriers to communication, such as physical or mental impairments, so try to adapt whatever you are saying to the actual customer and situation you find yourself in.

Tips

1. **Check you are being understood** with questions such as 'does that make sense?' and 'have I explained that properly?'

2. **Check out their body language**. Do they look bored or confused?

3. **Summarise the conversation**, which will give the customer a chance to clarify anything you may have got wrong

4. **Don't use jargon**. The chances are that your customer won't understand it.

5. **Talk about results** – sometimes the specific detail of what you do is less important than the tangible result that the customer experiences

Small Business Sales Dilemmas

Case Study

Roger worked in the technical department of a high-tech manufacturing firm developing state of the art components for clients in the medical, defence and aerospace industries. When an opportunity came up to help the sales team at an exhibition, he jumped at it. His manager explained that they needed someone with technical knowledge to answer customers' questions and thought Roger would be a perfect fit.

The exhibition was a large one and the company's stand got quite busy. The staff took it in turns to man the stand and answer questions.

Although Roger was not used to dealing with the public, he was thoroughly enjoying himself and got stuck in, helping wherever he could and supporting the sales staff with the technical side of things.

However, on the second day, he was on his own for a bit while one colleague was on a break and another was talking with an existing customer who came to visit the stand.

He was approached by a man who was taking an interest in some of the components on the stand. He began to ask Roger some questions. Enthusiastically, Roger began to explain all about how they were made, the testing processes, measurements, raw materials and statistics that he knew so well. He chatted for about 10 minutes before the man thanked him and walked off.

Straight away, another man came to the stand and asked about delivery times. Roger wasn't completely sure about this because he knew it varied according to workload, technical specification, delivery requirements and quite a lot of other factors, so he gave the man detailed information about all of this and more. The man looked a bit confused and asked if Roger could just give him a rough idea. Roger carefully explained again the factors that affected delivery schedules and availability and gave the man lots of extra information too. Roger didn't notice that the man was starting to look rather annoyed and kept on giving him more and more information.

At that point one of Roger's colleagues returned and took over the conversation. "Thank goodness" said the man – I'm sorry mate, but I didn't have a clue what you were talking about". He and Roger's colleague talked for a few minutes and then, with a cheery smile, he filled out his enquiry details and promised to be in touch.

It turned out that he was a major buyer for one of the companies that Roger's colleague had been trying to get into. However, Roger had so confused him that he had been on the verge of walking away from the stand. Fortunately, nothing had been lost and he was now interested again.

After that, they agreed that Roger was better suited to talking with other technically minded people and that the sales team would deal with the rest of the enquiries. This worked much better and Roger could talk freely and confidently about the work he loved to people who completely understood him.

16 - What tools could you use to stop and refocus a sales call?

Even with preparation, a business meeting can go wrong and you can feel as though you have lost either control or direction. Often, this is due to factors outside your control from a simple interruption like a phone ringing, or something more serious such as an evacuation. However, it can also be that the direction of the conversation veers off course and you find yourself a little lost about how to get it back.

When this happens, your flow and your momentum can be hard to recover. For your sales call to work effectively, it is vital that you can refocus quickly and smoothly.

Tips

1. **Always have an objective for the meeting.** That way, if you start to get lost, you can go back to your main objective

2. **Prioritise.** If the discussion starts to get too broad, you could say that it might not be possible to cover everything in one meeting and ask the customer which issue is their priority

3. **Summarise.** Using a summary of what you have discussed already is a great way to slow things down, review what has been discussed so far and give you time to think

4. **Make sure you are not talking too much.** Think about what questions you could ask the customer to get the conversation back on track

5. **Ask for a glass of water.** This creates a small breathing space for you to gather your thoughts and get back on track

Case Study

Sandra loved her job in sales and was good at it.

She had identified a potential client who was a good fit for her product – a high end telecoms system. She had an appointment booked with Tom, their Head of Facilities to discuss the project.

Sandra had been trained to always have a simple agenda for a meeting and to be prepared. So, as usual, she had her agenda, some brochures, a presentation and other potential resources at hand. She ran through the agenda with Tom and the meeting progressed smoothly. Tom was clearly interested in the product and was making positive responses to her questions. After about half an hour, Tom asked if one of his group leaders Craig, could come into the meeting too – on the basis that he would be one of the users of the system.

Like Tom, Craig seemed genuinely interested in Sandra's system.

Suddenly, they were interrupted by a member of staff who asked to speak to Tom. He left and Sandra and Craig could see that he had just been given some bad news. Craig excused himself and went to see what had happened.

He returned and explained that Tom's wife and baby had been in a car accident and were on their way to hospital. For obvious reasons, Tom would not be returning to the meeting. Craig didn't seem sure what to do next and he stood, rather uncomfortably near to Sandra.

Even though all the momentum had gone from the meeting, Sandra realised that she could still talk with Craig. Sensing that he was still unclear what to do, Sandra took the initiative and suggested that they take a short break and then continue with the meeting. Craig agreed and went off to sort out tea and coffee.

While he was gone, Sandra reviewed her agenda, gathered her thoughts and decided to what to do.

On Craig's return, Sandra suggested it would be helpful to give Craig an overview of what had been discussed before he had joined the meeting. He agreed and they spent another 30 minutes or so productively going over details of the project, clarifying lots of things about usage and requirements.

On her return to the office, Sandra made sure she sent a card to Tom and followed up the next day with a phone call. Fortunately, Tom's wife and baby had been discharged from hospital with only minor bruises.

A few days later, Tom called her to reschedule their meeting. He apologised, but Sandra could reassure him that Craig and herself had covered a lot of ground and had continued to explore the project in detail.

Indeed, later, Tom placed the order with Sandra and praised her for her professionalism in handling the unforeseen interruption and for using the time with Craig to really understand the company's issues and requirements.

17 - How can you encourage yourself to sell when you feel demotivated?

Sometimes it can be hard to reach out to potential customers. Perhaps you have had a lot of rejection, or you have just increased your prices, a customer has been giving you a hard time, or you are just plain and simple not 'in the mood'.

One of the characteristics of successful sales people is that they know how to keep going even when they don't really feel like it. These people know how to motivate themselves and get going whatever the circumstances.

Tips

1. **You will always have good days and bad days** – try to remember that the bad ones will pass

2. **Make sure you always have alternatives** – if you concentrate on one big project and it doesn't work out, at least you'll have something else to focus on

3. **Give yourself time** – perhaps do something else important but easier to do until you feel better

4. **Read through testimonials from happy customers** – it is one of the best 'pick me ups'

5. **Keep going** – you never know what is just around the corner

Case Study

Ian and Darren worked in the customer service team of a software company. They handled complaints and queries and passed enquiries to the sales team.

They knew which people in the sales team were better at dealing with particular enquiries and tried their best to match callers and salespeople as well as possible.

One day, Ian asked Darren if he knew what was wrong with Stella, one of their top salespeople. He had noticed that recently she had been less enthusiastic than normal. Also, her figures were dropping. Darren thought he knew the reason – she had lost a big deal that would have earned her loads of commission and she was struggling to bounce back from it. Both men decided that for the time being, it might be worth passing leads to other members of the team, rather than Stella, to ensure that the leads were closed.

Nothing much happened until 2 weeks later. Stella came in and she was just like her old self. She knuckled down to work and started ringing potential customers. She also got in touch with Darren and asked if any leads had come in. He had one lead he had intended to give to someone else, but Stella was so buoyant that he gave it to her instead.

Stella was a picture of enthusiasm and hard work that week. She literally worked every minute she could and seemed to be genuinely happy.

Ian decided he was going to ask her what had happened to make this change happen. When he got the chance to speak to her, she explained.

"I really expected to win that big deal and it took me a while to accept that I hadn't. It knocked the stuffing out of me to be honest. But sales is a funny old game. Sometimes you have highs and sometimes you have lows – so if you like and accept the good bits, you must accept the bad bits too. Anyway, last week I went home and read through some testimonials from happy customers. I also had a look at all the awards I have won and pictures from holidays I had paid for by being good at sales and I realised how much I had to be grateful for. Anyway, I decided I had better just get on with things, so I did. Good thing I did – 2nd call I made today, I got a really big order, so it was all worth it!"

18 - Sales funnels – are you using one of the simplest tools to sell more?

There are lots of tools to help you sell more, but one of the simplest is called a Sales Funnel. The great thing about it is that you can make one quickly and easily with just a pen and a bit of paper. Many people find a Sales Funnel a great tool not only because it is very effective, but because it is visual – you can put it on your notice board and use it to identify who is likely to purchase your goods and services, without going to the bother of investing in an expensive piece of software.

Tips

1. **Sales funnels are wide at the top and narrow at the bottom.** Keep feeding more suspects in at the top

2. **Use sticky notes** for ease of use – they can be moved around easily

3. **You can colour code the sticky notes** to indicate the lead source – a great way of identifying quickly which sources work the best

4. **You can use different sales funnels for different products** and have several on the go at the same time

5. **To get the best out of a sales funnel, it should be somewhere visible,** so you can see it all the time.

Case Study

Rachel managed a small sales and customer service team. When going through the figures, she realised that sales had plateaued somewhat over the last 3 months. So, she called a meeting to discuss what was going on. She asked every member of the team for input and it soon became clear that there were absolutely loads of leads but that they were not being chased up in an organised or methodical way. Also, depending on who she spoke to, some members of the team considered a lead to be a lead when it was really nothing more than a request for information, whereas other people should have been closing really hot leads, but failed to recognise that the customers were ready to buy.

Rachel decided to do some training on sales funnels for her team. She explained that a sales funnel is shaped like a real funnel – open at the top, then it gets narrower as it goes down. At the top lots of suspects go in, then by qualifying them, the suspects turn into prospects, leads and, eventually customers. At every stage of the process, people fall out the side (no longer interested, gone away, requirements changed, gone to a competitor). She explained the stages as follows:

1. **Suspects** – these are unknown to you – they might be just a name or the name of a company that you want to approach. No one knows if they need you or not.

2. **Prospects** – these are people or businesses who have engaged with you in some way – for example, you have spoken to them, they have visited your website or perhaps you met them at an event. You can initiate further contact with them to find out if they can move to the next stage, which is:

3. **Leads** – these are people who have a need for what you offer. It may not be straight away, in which case they are a 'warm' lead, but if they have an urgent need, they are called 'hot' leads and should be your primary focus

4. **Customers** – a customer is someone who has either bought from you or contracted to buy from you

Rachel got her entire team to make up some sales funnels and go through all their records, categorising all their contacts into these four definitions, using Post-It notes so that the contacts could easily be moved into different bands if things changed.

As a result, it soon became clear where the focus should be and Rachel's team started by concentrating on the hottest leads, which was successful.

Rachel explained that they must continue to put suspects in the top of the sales funnel, as at every stage, some of these potential customers always fall out.

After just 2 weeks, there was a dramatic increase in orders, simply by being organised and using sales funnels effectively. Even better, the staff loved the simplicity of them and the immediacy so continued to use them effectively from then on.

19 - How good are you at keeping customer records?

However large or small your organisation, you should have some sort of record system in place to keep information about your clients and potential clients. There are lots of ways of doing this, from buying a sophisticated CRM (Customer Relationship Management) package to simply keeping a simple manual filing system. To some extent, the method does not matter, but what is important is that you can trace and use information quickly and effectively.

Tips

1. **Have some sort of system** – it doesn't matter what, but make sure you have something

2. **There are lots of options** – choose one that fits your needs and your business

3. **If you have invested in a system, make sure you use it.** It is only as good as the information you put into it

4. **Get as much information as possible**, but as a minimum, you need: name, telephone, email, company name and address. Also leave a space to take notes.

5. **Keep it up to date** – although people do tend to keep the same personal email address, other information can go out of date quickly.

Case Study

Susan was a wonderful illustrator and she had a core of regular clients who came to use her skills at her local business centre. She also got quite a lot of walk-in trade from the other businesses there and benefitted from a local networking group who met there once a month.

Everything was fine, until the owners of the building decided to sell it to a developer and Susan, who only had a few months left on her business lease was given notice to quit.

Almost overnight, the number of customers dropped, as tenants in the building focussed on finding somewhere new and the networking group stopped coming.

Susan decided to contact all her clients to make sure that she kept as many of them as possible before she moved. However, she was not very organised and a lot of her clients' details were just stored on her phone under their first names. She had some email addresses and a few telephone numbers but that was all.

Her plans of sending "change of address" cards to all her clients was going to be a problem – she only had a handful of addresses.

She sat down and started to go through her messy paperwork, trying to find business cards, invoices, scraps of paper; anything to identify her valuable clients. A friend showed her how to take a picture on her Android device which saved business cards and gradually she began to find the information she needed. As well as storing data on her phone, she bought a simple set of postcards and an A-Z index and started to fill out as many details as she could.

As well as existing customers, Susan also discovered lots of enquiries from potential customers, so could create a separate list of people to try and convert into paying customers. Because of all this work, she could start a simple email campaign, write to everyone about her move and include a money off voucher.

Rather to her surprise, once she had her card system up and running, it was easy to administer. She backed it up on her phone too and so could get in touch much more simply than before, when she had just relied on people contacting her.

It took a while, but eventually she could replace all her lost customers. Her new system meant that she was much more responsive too and could follow up on enquiries better. Finally, she enjoyed keeping control of her record system – a bonus she had not expected.

20 - Are you using the Power of Follow-up?

Following-up is the process of continuing to contact potential customers. It is particularly important to use follow-up, because statistics show that the majority of sales are not made on the 1st, 2nd, 3rd or even 4th contact with prospects. In fact, they are more normally made somewhere between the 5th and 12th contact. Obviously, these figures will vary depending on the sector and what you are selling, but it is a good starting point.

Tips

1. **Remember most sales are made on the 5th – 12th follow up**, so keep trying

2. **Use a variety of follow up methods** – you never know which one will work for you and you might lose the sale by not using it.

3. **Plan to follow up** – then you are much more likely to do it

4. **Don't be a stalker!** Spread out your follow ups over days, weeks and months – you are playing a long-term game

5. **Don't be scared** – the worst that can happen is that they say 'no'!

Case Study

Toni ran a bespoke cake making service, creating beautiful personalised cakes for special occasions. She was often very busy at times like Christmas, Easter and Valentine's day, but throughout the rest of the year, business could be erratic and her cash flow fluctuated from month to month.

May was a particularly quiet month and it was clear Toni was going to struggle to pay her bills.

She was due to go to a regular networking meeting and knew that one of the members was a sales trainer, so she rang her and asked her advice.

The trainer asked what Toni did with enquiries. Toni explained that these were all kept on a memo pad, but the memo slips were scattered everywhere. The sales trainer then gave her some very simple advice:

"Find all of your enquiry slips. Sort them out into people who used you and people who didn't. Then follow up the ones who didn't."

She also told Toni to use a variety of different methods and to contact everyone at least once a month, every month.

Once Toni had found all the memo slips she realised that she had over 150 enquiries from people who had not ended up using her. She calculated that if she rang 8 people every day, then it would take her about a month to contact all of them. She worked out what to say – nothing complicated, but along the lines of

"Hello, this is Toni from Toni's Cakes, you contacted us a while ago regarding (whatever their enquiry was about). I wondered, what is the situation now - are you still interested?"

Armed with this simple strategy, Toni methodically started to work through her list. After only one week, she had picked up 3 definite orders and 2 new quotes. Also, because she had asked everyone she spoke to if she could put them on her mailing list, she now had 30 people on record that she could contact next month by email.

The following month, Toni put together a simple newsletter, featuring pictures of cakes and emailed it to her new list of prospects. Within 24 hours of the newsletter going out, she had taken 4 more enquiries about bespoke cakes.

Over the next few months, Toni continued to use the follow up strategy, adding new enquiries as they came in and varying how she contacted people. Slowly but surely, her sales continued to grow. After 12 months, she did some analysis and realised that most of her new sales had come from people that she had contacted at least 6 times. She didn't need any more convincing and continued to use the follow up strategy with great success as a highly effective but non-pushy way of bringing in sales.

21 - Are you 'touching' your prospects enough?

Most sales are not made the first or second time you and a prospect are in contact. Depending on the sector and market, most sales are made somewhere between the fifth and twelfth time the customer and you make contact (touches).

Waiting for a customer to come to you can be a waste of time – other things come along to distract them, or they simply forget, so regularly following up helps them to remember you and what you are offering.

Vary your approach i.e. telephone, email, social media, direct mail, handwritten notes or free samples. This way you have the chance to add value and you reach them in the way that suits them the best.

Tips

1. **Remember 7 'touches'** is the average amount of times you need to contact a prospect before they turn into a customer

2. **Don't be a stalker** – don't call or email every day, but do keep consistently reminding them about you and your service

3. **You won't seem pushy** – even though you might worry about it, the customer is very unlikely to think you are, as long as you are professional

4. **Vary your approach** – use different way to get in touch and try and be creative to get their attention

5. **This is not a quick fix** – but it is a good way of converting prospects, so is a good technique when you are looking for longer term business.

Case Study

Jackeline worked in a multi-level marketing organisation selling top of the range health and beauty products. They were very well respected within the industry and Jackeline loved the products – she used them herself and knew everything necessary to sell them.

She conscientiously attended networking events, contacted friends and potential clients and distributed leaflets. She followed company guidelines on presentations and her technical knowledge of the products was excellent. She worked very hard and yet, after 4 months she had only made 2 sales and was on the verge of giving up.

Her manager sat her down to talk to her. Very gently, she asked Jackeline to explain exactly how she went about trying to win new customers. She discovered that Jackeline would make the initial contact, follow up and then….do absolutely nothing! After some probing, Jackeline revealed that after the initial follow up, she didn't do any more because she didn't want to seem pushy.

She was worried that she might annoy people or that they might think she was a nuisance and that they would not then buy from her.

Jackeline's manager could explain that lots of research had been done on follow-up and the 'optimum' amount of times people needed to 'touch' prospects before they decided to buy. The generally understood amount of times customers needed contact was 7. It did of course vary according to the industry and what was being sold, so sometimes it could be the first or second time and sometimes it could mean a prospect needed to be contacted (touched) 20 times. But eventually, if there was a genuine need or desire, then by following up regularly, most people decided to buy when the time was right for them.

She gave Jackeline some strategies, specifically to follow up regularly, use different methods and to remember not to take any rejections personally. She also reminded Jackeline that it was very unlikely anyone was going to consider her pushy or annoying, as long as she was sensible and didn't try ringing constantly and made sure she focussed on value. She suggested Jackeline aimed for at least 10 touches before giving up.

Although it was slow, Jackeline was pleased to see that her manager's advice was good – gradually her persistence paid off and, over the following months, she started to get order after order. She never had to be pushy and no one told her that she was annoying – they just placed their orders in their own good time.

22 - Are you looking after your existing customers well enough?

The most profitable customers are those who are already using you. Although figures vary, it seems that the common consensus is that it costs between 4 and 10 times more to get a new customer than it does to keep an existing one.

Therefore, it makes sense to focus your attention on people or businesses that have already made the decision to use you. Of course, it is good to get new customers too, but not at the expense of those who are already loyal.

Tips

1. **Make sure your existing customers feel valued** – too many companies make a sale then don't follow up in any way.

2. **Create special deals and exclusive offers** – make them available for existing customers and not just new ones

3. **Take the trouble to speak to existing customers** – when was the last time you asked how they were finding your product or service, or simply just took the time to ask for their opinion?

4. **Create special clubs or social media groups just for customers** – this is a cheap and effective way to keep them in the loop and update them on things

5. **Use surveys** – from time to time, ask customers to complete a formal survey – it can be a great source of information about what you are doing well and what you need to improve.

Case Study

Mirabelle ran a networking group in the Home Counties. She had taken it over from her friend Ian, who had grown it from an initial base of 6 friends, to a thriving group which regularly had about 25 people attending. Due to ill-health, Ian wanted to take a step back and concentrate on recuperating.

Mirabelle could see the potential of the group and set about marketing it locally. She wanted to expand it and run both an evening and a day time group. To boost membership, she started by promoting a special reduced rate joining fee, where members could join for a year but only pay for 9 months. She got some new brochures printed, ran some adverts in the local press and generally invested a big chunk of time and energy in promoting the networking group to potential new customers.

It was successful and she got 6 new members in the first 2 months. However, some of the existing members heard about the discount and approached Mirabelle to find out if they too could enjoy the reduced rate when their membership was up for renewal. Mirabelle explained that it was a special introductory rate for new members only. It would not apply to renewals. There was a bit of moaning, but she stuck to her guns and pointed out that new membership was good for everyone as it provided more opportunities to do business.

Nothing more was said and Mirabelle continue to recruit new members – another 2 joined in the following month. She was disappointed that one of the existing members failed to renew, but as she was still 7 people up, she was not too concerned.

However, the following month she had a shock. The original group of 6 friends were all due to renew that month. One by one, they got in touch to say they were leaving. When pushed, they said that they didn't feel the new introductory rate was fair because the newcomers were getting all the benefits of the established group. The original 6 had worked hard to build it from nothing, yet they were being charged more than these people who had not contributed.

Worse was to come; without these original 6, the dynamic of the networking group started to change and, over the next 3 months, although Mirabelle got another 4 people to join, she lost the same amount.

She had worked so hard to build the group, she had spent money promoting it and yet, she had the same number of members as before, only now they were paying less money. Too late, she realised that she had failed to appreciate her existing members. A series of hurried phone calls followed. Mirabelle apologised to all the members who had left and asked if they wanted to return at a special rate. However, it was too late – the damage was done and she never got any of them to return.

23 - How can you upsell better?

Upselling is where you try to get a customer to buy something in addition to the primary purchase (thereby making the primary purchase more expensive). For example, if a customer buys a torch, you might suggest batteries, or they are considering buying your standard package and upgrade to a better and more expensive one. Upselling relates directly to the item purchased and the chances are that the customer will genuinely need or want these additional things.

Tips

1. **Make sure the customer is aware** of the upsell options and that they are easy to choose

2. **Draw customers in with the cheapest package first** and then provide the better value options

3. **Customers understand the difference between a cheap option and good value**, so by offering a choice they are more likely to be satisfied

4. **Try and use upselling options that delivery high value** to the customer, but don't cost you too much, thus increasing your margins

5. **Consider naming the different packages or options** to provide clarity to the customer

Case Study

Harris and Stella ran a holiday home in a beautiful part of the Cotswolds. They kept it open for 8 months of the year and for the winter months, they closed. There was a lot of competition for tourists locally, but usually they operated at near capacity so they could earn a reasonable living from their business.

However, there was not much left over for extras. They needed a new car and they had not been on holiday themselves for more than 4 years. In addition, as customers could search for holiday homes on the Internet, they knew their home lost out sometimes on price, as they tended towards the higher end of the price scale.

One day, Harris saw an article about BMW and how they used something called Upselling to increase their revenue. It gave him an idea. He explained to Stella

"When customers want to buy a new BMW, they can go onto the website and choose all the bits they want themselves. So, by the time they've chosen everything just how they would like it, the cost is often a lot higher, but of course, they get exactly what they want, so usually just pay. I think we could do something like that with the holiday home."

Together, Harris and Stella studied lots of different websites with many different upsell options and gradually worked out how they could apply this strategy in their business.

They came up with 3 different packages; standard (basically what they were offering now) Deluxe (which was about 8% more); with lots of extras such as the option to cancel, daily linen check, a voucher for reduced price meals at 3 local restaurants and a dog sitting voucher for the local dog walker). Then the Super Deluxe included all the above, but also a daily clean of the home, fresh flowers and use of Harris and Stella's hot tub which was in the adjacent garden and could easily be screened off as though it was part of the holiday home. This final option added another 22% to the price.

They put the 3 options on the website, made sure potential customers could select the option they preferred and started to monitor what happened over the year.

It was clear from the beginning that it was working, as about half the bookings chose either the Deluxe or the Super Deluxe. Harris and Stella kept a close eye on their costs, but by the end of the year they could easily see that the experiment had been a success. Overall, their turnover was up by about 14% and their costs had only increased by 3%.

In conclusion, they worked out that customers were drawn in by the cheapest option, but when they saw the genuine extra value in the more expensive packages, they often decided to upgrade. For them, upselling was a huge success.

24 - If you don't know your target, how will you know if you've achieved it?

If you are employed in sales, you will almost certainly have some sort of sales target to meet. However, lots of smaller businesses don't have a formal target – instead they have a much vaguer "I need to keep earning more" mind-set, which is not very helpful. Of course, that is fine when things are going well, but what about when things are tougher and business is hard to come by?

There is a well-known phrase "If you fail to plan, you plan to fail."

Take heed! The use of sensible sales targets can really help you grow your business more effectively and with more control.

Tips

1. **"If you fail to plan, you plan to fail"** - have some sort of target in place, even if you are not sure it is the right one (you can always change it later)

2. **Break down your targets into manageable chunks** – weekly or monthly for example.

3. **Review regularly** – if your target is too high it may not be achievable, or if it is too low, you may be missing out on opportunities

4. **There will be fluctuations** – for example, some businesses are affected by seasonal events (Christmas, holidays, weather) so adjust your targets to reflect this

5. **If you miss your target one month, don't panic** – just start again the next month – consistency is the key to long term success.

Small Business Sales Dilemmas

Case Study

Heather had been asked by her life coach friend Maureen to help her sort out her cash flow. She was stuck in a cycle of too busy and then too quiet, which also meant that she never had a steady income, because her earnings fluctuated so wildly.

Heather had experience of running a business and so sat down with Maureen to see if she could help. She asked lots of questions about her business – what she charged and how many clients she had, as well as details about her business overheads and living costs.

It soon became clear that Maureen had very little structure in place, so Heather took her right back to basics

- How much did she want to earn?
- How many clients did she have?
- What was the average each client paid?

Once Maureen had worked out this information, Heather asked her to do a simple sum

Target yearly earnings divided by the average paid by each client.

In Maureen's case, she wanted to earn £25,000 and her average client paid around £600. Heather asked her to work out how many clients she needed to achieve £25,000 and it turned out to be approximately 40.

Next, Heather told Maureen to divide that number by 12 to get a monthly target. It turned out that Maureen needed to get roughly 4 new clients every month.

Heather explained that by having a simple monthly target in place and ensuring that she achieved it every month, Maureen would have control over her earnings and her cash flow. Of course, some months she might get less clients and some months more, but the important thing was to do everything reasonably possible to get her 4 each month. Then, if she needed to earn more, or her circumstances changed, she could adjust her targets to suit her needs.

After just 3 months of trying this new system Maureen experienced lots of unexpected benefits. Not only had her income stabilised, but she realised that she was finding it much easier to plan her coaching activities, her marketing and her administration because she knew exactly how much work was coming in. Every 6 months, she reviewed her figures and could achieve a much better work life balance.

25 - How can you ensure that you will gain your prospect's trust?

Trust can take a long time to earn and can be lost very quickly. It is the same in personal relationships as it is in business – once you trust someone, you are much more likely to want to spend time with them and listen to what they say. However, trust can be elusive and many people are naturally suspicious of someone who is selling, so you need to both demonstrate and reinforce your reliability and credibility.

Tips

1. **If you say you are going to do it, then do it!** Don't muck around, delay or forget. The customer is waiting and your failure to do the thing you promised is a breach of trust.

2. **Never, never lie.** If you are not sure, then say you are not sure and offer to find out. Most people can spot a lie anyway, so it really is a waste of time.

3. **Use case studies and testimonials.** These provide reassurance that someone else has been there first and that everything worked out OK. This is particularly important if you are a small business or a start-up as you haven't had time to establish your reputation

4. **Ask customers what they think.** Do surveys or ask how they found dealing with you. If they complain, apologise and try to do better next time. Let them know what you are doing. Effective communication can be a great way of building trust

5. **Don't promise if you know you can't deliver.** If they want it in 24 hours and you know it's going to take 48 hours, then don't be tempted to pretend otherwise. Tell them the truth and often it will still be OK. Much better than delivering it late and finding out they have been moaning about you and further spoiling your reputation.

Case Study

Kevin was an experienced salesperson within the reprographics industry. He regularly achieved his target and was well respected. As the year ended, he was a front runner to be top salesperson in the country, with a prestigious holiday and bonus to be won if he achieved it.

He had one existing customer who he knew might be able to place a substantial order just before the year end. Whilst nothing was guaranteed, there was a good chance that, if this order was placed, Kevin would win his prize. Being a good salesman, he arranged for a visit to see this customer.

The customer had dealt with Kevin regularly over the years and knew he could provide good work on time and to the required standard. However, this would potentially be the biggest money value order he had ever placed with Kevin.

Before the meeting, Kevin prepared. He went through his notes, checked what the customer had liked and tried to work out if there were any weaknesses in his proposal. He made sure he had something he could use to reassure the customer for any potential objection.

At the meeting itself, Kevin tried to put his nerves to one side and concentrate on his customer's needs, as he had been trained to do. He didn't rush – instead, he took time to ask good open questions about the importance of the project and what the customer required of him. He summarised, checked, questioned and took care not to pressurise his customer.

When the customer raised some concerns, Kevin was ready with a testimonial which addressed the exact same issue. He knew all his figures and, although there was one thing he couldn't do for the customer, he was very open about it and had an alternative ready, which was acceptable to his customer.

There was one unexpected question about the specification of something rather technical. Kevin admitted he didn't know the answer, but made a phone call there and then to the production facility. They answered it simply and quickly which reassured the customer completely.

When Kevin asked for the order, the customer immediately said yes, happy that his project was in safe hands. When Kevin got back to the office and worked out the exact specification of the project, he was delighted to discover that it was an even bigger order than he had expected. He put the order through, confident that he should have done enough to win salesperson of the year.

26 - When is a sale not a sale?

Many people who are new to sales experience the frustration of thinking they have made a sale, but then, when it comes to the delivery of the product or service, confirmation in writing, or payment of a deposit, the customer does not seem to be able to finalise things and get going.

It can be difficult to work out what has happened and can feel awkward re-approaching the customer to say the equivalent of "what is happening then?".

Tips

1. **Have a formal process in place**, which might include a contract

2. When a sale has been agreed and the delivery of the product or service is not immediate, it is normal to **put everything in writing** and then both parties know exactly what to expect

3. **Has the customer said 'yes'?** Make sure that when you close, you have not misinterpreted what they said. For example, they might mean 'yes, but not for 6 months' which makes a considerable difference.

4. If a deposit is needed and they haven't paid the deposit, then do not start work until they have!

5. If they said 'yes' and then you can't get hold of them, they may have reconsidered going ahead.

Case Study

Craig ran a furniture removal business in the East of England. He only had two removal vans, so frequently experienced periods when he was fully booked and also periods when both vans and his staff were quiet.

His normal terms and conditions stated that a deposit was payable, but with regular clients or people he already knew, he sometimes agreed different payment terms if they asked. This normally worked out fine, so he wasn't unduly worried.

However, things changed entirely during a particularly busy period. A previous customer rang to make a booking for both vans. There was only one day Craig had any availability, so the customer asked to reserve that day. As he had paid with no trouble previously, Craig agreed when the customer asked to pay a minimum deposit of £100, with the balance of £5,300 to be paid on the day of the removal. He took the verbal booking as confirmation instead of asking the customer to complete a booking form.

The day before the removal was scheduled, Craig had not received any further correspondence or payment, so he tried to call the customer on the phone. There was no reply. He left messages, but no one called him back.

Craig now had a dilemma; should he have his vans and his staff on standby or not? Worse, he had turned down two other potential bookings on that day. If his customer didn't show, then he was potentially down by over five thousand pounds.

On the morning of the removal, Craig had still not heard anything. He realised that it was very unlikely that the customer now needed him. Nevertheless, he had to pay his staff for their time. Worse, he had no alternative work to offer them.

A few weeks later, he heard that this customer's business had gone into liquidation, owing thousands to local suppliers.

A hard lesson was learned and Craig made sure that every customer completed a booking form and paid in advance. There would no longer be any exceptions. Although there were a lot of complaints, genuine customers understood. Craig stuck to his new rules and, to his relief, never experienced this expensive situation again.

27 - How do you know if a customer is giving you buying signals?

One of the most difficult things to learn when selling is how to recognise buying signals. When a customer is in a state of mind to buy, they will give out clues – either verbal or non-verbal. Similarly, if they are not ready to buy yet, then they will, through their body language and what they say to you, be either directly or indirectly telling you this.

The trick is to be able to read this information accurately and to act accordingly. You will also need to consider factors such as whether they are under pressure at a particular moment (for example because they are trying to meet a deadline and you are delaying them!) or whether they are saying one thing and their body language tells you something else.

Tips

1. **It becomes easier to read buying signals with experience,** so don't worry if it seems difficult to begin with

2. **Try and concentrate on verbal signals to begin with** - are the easiest to read and respond to

3. **Check out simple non-verbal signals, like whether the person is smiling or looks worried** – these are self-explanatory

4. **Put yourself in your customer's shoes** – there might be something else going on that has nothing to do with you, so be sensitive to things outside your influence

5. **Just ask** - if you think something is wrong, or the customer is unhappy about something, trust your instinct and ask them about it – much better than just guessing and getting it wrong

Case Study

Samantha loved making jams and chutneys and had developed a range of delicious recipes. With the encouragement of her husband she spent money on converting her garage into a proper kitchen and as the summer fruit season arrived, began working in earnest to produce her range of preserves.

She had never really thought beyond developing recipes and making the preserves and soon she had a huge collection. However, she had absolutely no idea how to go about attracting customers.

She decided to try the range on her friends first, so she had a little informal gathering at her house and just let everyone sample what she had done. The results were amazing – used to mass produced shop jam, Samantha's products tasted wonderful and her friends said so. Several people asked how much they were, but Samantha pointed out that she wasn't ready to sell them yet. One of them begged her, but she said 'no'. Her friend made her promise to tell her as soon as they were ready and, reluctantly Samantha agreed.

Samantha did a couple more trial tasting sessions and got similar results every time. However, as she wasn't 100% confident yet of her recipes and the presentation of the jams, she put people off, when they asked about buying. She promised that she would let them know when she was ready.

Summer turned to autumn and Samantha continued cooking. Many of her recipes used fruit from the old fruit trees in her garden, so she wanted to make use of the time she had to make her produce.

However, things changed suddenly one day. Her husband, invited over some friends who had been at the original tasting. Samantha made scones and brought out a selection of her preserves to eat with them.

"Oh, here is Samantha's secret jam again!" joked her friend.
"What do you mean?" asked her husband.
"Didn't you know – she never sells it, she just teases us with how delicious it is and then keeps it all to herself! She's terrible!"

Samantha blushed and explained that it wasn't quite ready yet and she didn't know quite how much to charge and she would get in touch when the time was right.

"Nonsense" declared her husband – she's got a whole room full of the stuff. How much would you be prepared to pay for a jar? We'll sort you out now?"

The friend said she thought £4 or £5 would be fair. So, with Samantha protesting, they went into her store room to see what was in there. In the end, her friend bought 4 jars. Samantha couldn't believe it!

Word soon got out and, within 2 days she had sold about 20 jars. She began to realise that her friends were not 'just being polite' as she had thought – they wanted to buy her preserves. With her husband's encouragement, she contacted all the people who had expressed an interest in buying and soon her products were flying off the shelf, as people bought, tasted and enjoyed her unique products. She learned a valuable lesson – if people say they want to buy from you, then that is the best buying signal of all.

28 - Do you have too many toxic customers?

Most business people would say they need more customers, but the fact is that some customers might be sapping both your energy and your bank balance if they are not a good fit for what you do.

Ideal clients will support your long-term business growth, but toxic customers (in other words, customers who are difficult to work with, who sap your energy and who are constantly negative) will do the opposite. Therefore, it is a good plan to only encourage those customers who are a good fit and to be ruthless about discouraging those customers who would dilute your hard-won brand and reputation.

Tips

1. **Work out who your ideal client is,** then it is easier to spot the ones who are not a good fit

2. **Look out for general negativity** – does the person moan, complain and criticise with no justification? Then they might be toxic for you.

3. **Do not be tempted to take money now** – play the long-term game – a negative review can do long-lasting damage to your reputation

4. **Perhaps you should cull some of your existing customers** – it is a good exercise to go through all your customers from time to time and see if you should get rid of any who take up too much of your time and effort.

5. **Don't mistake genuine need or pain as automatically being toxic behaviour** – sometimes a customer has been badly let down and is experiencing genuine worry which you could fix. If your gut tells you that you are a good fit for each other, then you probably are!

Case Study

Elaine had a thriving training business. She helped teach social marketing skills to small businesses and entrepreneurs and had steadily been growing for 3 years. Eventually, she got to the stage where she needed an assistant to help with her workload. She recruited Adam, an enthusiastic graduate who wanted to gain some sales experience.

Adam's role was to introduce potential customers to Elaine, who would then assess if they were a good fit and then hopefully sign them up as customers.

Adam settled in quickly – Elaine had a good reputation locally and this made his job very straightforward. He passed loads of potential leads to Elaine and she could close a great deal of them.

One day, Adam passed on a lead to Elaine from a man he had met at a networking meeting. Elaine duly spoke to the man but he didn't sign up. Adam was surprised because he had been enthusiastic about doing the training. He asked Elaine what went wrong.

Instead of answering directly, Elaine sat him down and asked him some questions about how he had met the man. She then told him that this customer was not a good fit. In fact, worse than that, he was potentially quite a toxic customer. Adam was genuinely confused – how could Elaine describe such an enthusiastic potential customer in these terms?

Elaine explained that the man had been quite rude on the phone. Although that wasn't necessarily a problem in itself, he then went on to be quite negative about people he had worked with and even a previous course he had been on. She also realised that he didn't listen properly to what Elaine had been saying and had got a couple of important pieces of information wrong, because he hadn't been concentrating.

She told Adam that, in her experience, people like this were often very negative within a group environment and could easily bring down the entire mood of the class. Not only that, but they tended to give poor feedback. In other words, they spoiled the experience of genuine students (which meant that the overall feedback was worse). She had noticed too that this type of personality could often consume a lot of her time and energy – asking irrelevant questions, interrupting and always wanting to get extra advice for free, whether or not it was convenient.

The bottom line was that this person was not a good fit for her culture and her brand and, although the money would have been nice, she had to take the long-term view that she was better off without him. Far better to let him go to a competitor and free her up to serve the customers who were a good fit for her.

29 - How well do you know your competitors?

It is inevitable that there will be competition for your business – either directly (where others offer a similar service) or indirectly where there are other things competing for customers' money. However, if you take the time to understand what your competitors are doing, you will be able to ensure that your own offering is competitive and hopefully you will attract your ideal customers to you.

Tips

1. **Check out competitors' websites** and see how they compare to yours. Ask yourself "If I was a customer, who would I choose?"

2. **Ring up your competitors to make an enquiry** – it will show you how they deal with enquires too and you may pick up some tips

3. **Look at competitors' testimonials** – what makes their customers happy? Is that something you could do as well, perhaps even better?

4. **Create simple guarantees.** Maybe your guarantee is hidden deep in your terms and conditions. If so, make sure it is displayed clearly on your website or on marketing material.

5. **Keep up to date** – check your competitors regularly – the chances are that information will change and it is good to be up to date

Case Study

Aidan was really struggling with his decluttering business. He absolutely loved what he did, but he was failing to convert enquiries into sales and was worried that he might have to give up.

In desperation, he contacted a friend who had approached him to declutter her house. In the end, she hadn't used him. He decided to ask her out for a coffee to find out why.

As Aidan's good friend, Rita was more than happy to meet with him and to help him.

She listened carefully as Aidan asked her for her honest feedback about why she hadn't used his decluttering services.

She explained that, although she knew Aidan well, she had got 2 other quotes as well, because she wasn't familiar with the options available. Both other companies had asked her lots of questions to really uncover what it was that she wanted and both had sent a uniformed member of staff around to assess her house. The first company was about the same price as Aidan, but had loads of happy customer testimonials, came with a guarantee that if she wasn't happy, she could have as many extra decluttering sessions as she wanted and followed up every 2 days or so to see if she was ready to go ahead. She had chosen this company

The second, more expensive option offered the same, but with a deep clean service too. Rita hadn't wanted that, but like the first company, they kept in touch with her regularly until she confirmed she was going to use someone.

Rita kindly pointed out that Aidan had come to her house, but hadn't asked nearly as many questions about what she wanted and what she was trying to achieve. He had no customer testimonials (and she had checked – there were none on his website either). Finally, he had given no indication of guarantees, follow up visits or anything. Although Aidan was her friend, he had not seemed as professional as the other company and she felt that they would do a better job.

Aiden sat quietly. He had all the things his competitors had, but he had not been advertising them. He had a uniform, but didn't use it when he went out to quote. He had a box full of enthusiastic testimonials from happy customers, but he never used them. He unofficially would always go back again if a customer wasn't happy. He also realised that he hardly ever followed up quotations because he didn't want to look pushy.

Coffee over, Aidan did some more research on what his competitors were offering. He also picked up some ideas from the way they spoke to him on the phone when he rang up (pretending to be interested in using their services).

With this information, in very little time, Aiden could improve the branding of his business. He made sure he was always uniformed, he used testimonials and written guarantees, he asked loads of questions and, most importantly he used his diary to follow up regularly. None of this cost anything, but straight away, he started to win more work.

30 - Are you selling ethically?

Ethics is the difference between doing right and wrong and it is about doing what is legally and morally right. So, when you are selling, it is important to sell ethically – in other words, be honest about your product or service and give your customer the right information. Tied in with this, you should be fair in your treatment of customers and ensure that you keep customer information confidential.

Whilst ethical selling protects the customer, there are also sound business reasons for adopting it – customers are much more likely to use you, come back again and recommend you to others if they know you operate within an ethical framework.

Tips

1. **Always tell the truth.** This means you cannot exaggerate, lie or hold back important information about your product or service that might stop the customer buying it

2. Don't make false promises – for example if you know delivery will take 3 days, don't tell the customer it will take one day just to get the sale

3. **Avoid the hard sell** – this is when you use high pressure tactics to secure a sale

4. **Don't lie about or try to discredit the competition** – for example, saying their products are poor quality when they are not

5. **Do not use bribery** – this includes payments, gifts or other incentives

Case Study

After 3 years of working as a gardener with a small local business, Paul decided he wanted to set up his own gardening business. He was frustrated because he felt like he was doing the hard work, but his employer was getting most of the money. Although he didn't have any clients, he knew that a few of the people he already did work for via his employer, were unhappy with the prices that they were being charged. His plan was to undercut his employer, whilst still providing the same service, guaranteeing that he would have some income to start with.

So, he left, got some leaflets printed and started to contact these clients. He got a mixed reaction – some knew him and were happy to continue to use him, but others said that they didn't want to change because they had a long relationship with the company.

Having a good knowledge of how his employer worked, Paul tried to persuade them to use him instead, by explaining some of the things that he felt his old employer had been doing wrong. He told customers that they were being overcharged, that sometimes they were paying for whole hours when the jobs were taking less than that. He also stretched the truth a bit when he said that some of the chemicals and treatments used were not the branded products that they were supposed to be.

To his surprise he met with quite a lot of resistance and didn't persuade many people, but at least he had a small core of customers to start work with. Some of them were quite difficult customers, but he didn't mind, as he confidently expected to grow fast.

Paul was keen to earn money as fast as possible. Whatever a customer wanted, he said he could do it. If they needed a big job doing, he dropped everything to do it.

However, he soon realised that this wasn't sustainable – to say yes to one urgent job, he realised he would have to let down two small but regular clients. He needed the money, so he did the urgent job and the regular clients were OK about it. So, when a similar situation arose again, he had no hesitation in accepting the big job.

That's when things started to go wrong. Both regular clients stopped using him. One said that he was not reliable enough and she was going to start using his old company again. The other just never returned his phone calls any more.

The turning point was when Paul quoted for another large job, confident that he would win it because of price, but when he did, he realised that he couldn't do it all by himself. He couldn't afford to employ help because he had priced himself too low and he wouldn't meet the deadline unless he cut corners. He did the job, but poorly and word started to spread about his unreliability.

Instead of his business growing, he lost even the small number of clients he already had. In the end, he gave up and asked for his old job back. However, by that time it was too late – his old employer didn't want him either, having been informed by his loyal customers of what Paul had tried to do.

31 - Are you using the simplest and best tool to manage your time?

Almost everyone struggles with time management – it is so much easier to do what you enjoy, rather than what is important or urgent. However, as an entrepreneur, if you don't focus on improving your time management skills, your whole business could suffer, as you fail to work on the key strategic issues. That could mean that you fail to grow and develop as you would wish, but it could be even more serious, leading to the collapse of the business

Tips

1. **Prepare the night before**, what key tasks you want to accomplish the next day

2. **Put the most important task first**

3. **Have a fixed number of tasks** – between 3 and 6 seems to work well for most people

4. **Be methodical** – do your tasks in order, not by which is easiest or most fun.

5. **Anything you cannot finish goes on to the next day's list**

Case Study

By 1918, Charles M. Schwab was one of the richest men in the world. He was the president of the Bethlehem Steel Corporation, the largest shipbuilder and the second-largest steel producer in America at the time. The famous inventor Thomas Edison once referred to Schwab as the "master hustler." He was constantly seeking an edge over the competition.

One day in 1918, in his quest to increase the efficiency of his team and discover better ways to get things done, Schwab arranged a meeting with a highly-respected productivity consultant named Ivy Lee, a successful businessman. The story is that Schwab brought Lee into his office and said, "Show me a way to get more things done."

"Give me 15 minutes with each of your executives," Lee replied.

"How much will it cost me," Schwab asked.

"Nothing," Lee said. "Unless it works. After three months, you can send me a check for whatever you feel it's worth to you."

The Ivy Lee Method

During his 15 minutes with each executive, Lee explained his simple method for achieving peak productivity:

1. At the end of each work day, write down the six most important things you need to accomplish tomorrow. Do not write down more than six tasks.

2. Prioritize those six items in order of their true importance.

3. When you arrive tomorrow, concentrate only on the first task. Work until the first task is finished before moving on to the second task.

4. Approach the rest of your list in the same fashion. At the end of the day, move any unfinished items to a new list of six tasks for the following day.

5. Repeat this process every working day.

The strategy sounded simple, but Schwab and his team tried it.

After three months, Schwab was so delighted with the progress his company had made that he called Lee into his office and wrote him a cheque for $25,000 (a $25,000 in 1918 is the equivalent of about $400,000 today).

The Ivy Lee Method is very simple, but that is one of the reasons it works – it is easy to stick to and if something crops up, easy to revisit and get back on track. It also forces you to make tough decisions – the very fact that you must impose a rule upon yourself means that you are committed to doing a certain thing and less likely to be distracted by everything else.

Also, it means there is not that awful barrier to starting – you are forced to decide on your tasks the night before and so when you begin work, that decision has already been made.

32 - Are you writing winning sales proposals?

Sales proposals are written documents which set out exactly what and how you will provide for your customer if they decide to buy your product or service. They are primarily used when the purchase is complex and/or the value of the purchase is high.

Developing and submitting a good proposal can mean the difference between winning a sale and not. After all, it is often the first tangible thing that the customer has had from you! Having said that, a Sales Proposal does not have to be complicated – what it must be is professional.

Tips

1. **First impressions count**. Your proposal should look professional and you should make it easy to follow and read

2. **Pay attention to the detail** – grammar, spelling, punctuation, consistency of fonts and formatting will make it look sharp and well presented – neglect these and it will just look sloppy

3. **Would you trust you?** Put yourself in your customer's shoes – if your proposal is not professional, then what does it imply about the professionalism of your company?

4. **Never, ever miss a deadline** – there are plenty of competitors out there who will get their proposal in on time. If you are late with yours, you are pretty much guaranteed not to be considered

5. **Check the detail** – if you do make a mistake and you win the deal, you may have to honour the contract even if it is to your detriment.

Case Study

The Big Sparkle was Susan's dream company. She had been running it for about 10 years, providing domestic cleaning services in her local area and had a reliable team of cleaners and a strong customer base.

Although business was steady, Susan was trying to get into the commercial cleaning sector, as the value of the contracts could be large. She had a great track record and lots of good testimonials from satisfied customers so, she started approaching local businesses and, straight away got a fair amount of interest.

She knew that pricing these contracts was more complicated than pricing up the cleaning of a house, but she soon realised that commercial customers expected a formal proposal, not just a quotation – they wanted to know exactly what was included and in detail.

The first proposal Susan wrote took her 6 hours and she nearly missed the deadline to submit it. She didn't get the work.

The next proposal took about the same time and, in a rush again, Susan submitted it without checking it over. To her delight, she got a phone call from her prospect the very next morning saying she had been the successful bidder. It was only once she started recruiting staff for the contract that she realised in her rush to submit it, she hadn't checked the figures properly and if she honoured the contract she would be making a loss of about £60 per week. She had to withdraw and the customer made it very clear that he wasn't happy about having his time wasted.

Over the next few weeks, Susan struggled to submit further proposals and didn't win one.

In the end, she decided she had to get help and she contacted a business consultant friend to give her some advice. The list of things Susan was doing wrong seemed endless – she didn't have a clear structure, her grammar was terrible, the breakdown of costings was difficult to understand. She didn't even put her contact details on one of the proposals she submitted. As her friend pointed out, they couldn't have used her even if they had wanted to.

Together her friend helped her create a standard template for proposals. It was professionally written and laid out and, with standard paragraphs in it, all that Susan had to do was tailor it to each individual customer. There were clear headings outlining the background to the proposal, customer problems and/or objectives, the scope of the contract, solution and benefits of using The Big Sparkle, together with clearly laid out pricing options and several clear but not pushy Calls to Action to get customers to contact her.

Once Susan started using the template, she reduced the average amount of time spent on each proposal to about 1 hour, but, more importantly, she started to win some contracts. She was achieving something like 1 in 3 conversions in the contracts she was pitching for. The proposal not only looked professional, but it was a valuable sales tool, helping her to sell her services professionally and persuasively to the commercial market.

33 - How can you overcome those days when you feel overwhelmed?

Everyone has days when it can be hard to work on the things you need to and selling is no exception, particularly as it can be demotivating to experience lots of potential customers saying no or telling you they are not interested. As entrepreneurs and small business owners, there can be the additional factor of being isolated and not being able to share experiences with other people.

Tips

1. **Remind yourself of your big strategic goals** and why you are doing what you are doing

2. **Allocate time away from the day to day running of the business** – if you don't, you will end up dealing with the small stuff

3. **Remind yourself of what you have achieved already** – a good tip is to read testimonials and good reviews from happy customers

4. **Share!** – don't keep your worries and troubles to yourself. Find someone you trust – friend, family or even business coach and talk things through. It can be immensely helpful to just talk things through

5. **Delegate** – if there is anything you can possibly give to another member of staff or outsource, then do so – the increased productivity and freeing up of your time often means it is worth far more than the actual money you pay.

Small Business Sales Dilemmas

Case Study

Stuart was struggling. He had taken over the family business when his parents retired and he was feeling overwhelmed. A large customer had relocated recently, meaning they lost that business and overall turnover was down by about 12% year on year. He had less money to spend on marketing and he felt he was not converting enough enquiries into sales. Despite that, the bills seemed to be mounting up, he had staff reviews to do, some new machinery to buy and, at home, his wife was expecting their 4th child. He felt completely ragged. Although he had once looked forward to taking over the business, he had come to the realisation that he wasn't quite sure why he had wanted it.

In desperation, he rang his parents and got through to his mother.

She listened to him, before carefully explaining that she was going to ask him some questions and he was to go away and write down the answers. The questions were:

- "What is your vision for the business?"
- "What is the company brilliant at doing?"
- "What sort of growth would you like to achieve in the next year?"
- "What personal goals do you have? How can the company help you achieve them?"
- "What one big new thing would you like the company to be able to do?"
- "What tasks cause you the most headaches?"

She told Stuart that there were no right or wrong answers, but he must give himself time to think about them properly. She offered to come down for one day to stand in for him while he worked it all out. He accepted gratefully.

Stuart realised that the questions were all about going back to basics. He took himself off to a local coffee shop, turned off his phone and sat there with a blank note book, a pen and loads of post-it notes. He stayed there all day.

With the freedom to think about what mattered, instead of fire-fighting, Stuart started to objectively look at the business. He reconnected with the aims and objectives of the company. He realised that he had once had some big plans to drive the business forward, but had got distracted by the loss of his large customer. He also realised that he knew exactly what to do to grow the other accounts and to bring in more customers and a lot of his problems were caused by dealing with day to day things instead of working on the overall strategy. He had been working in the business instead of on the business

As this realisation dawned, Stuart started to change from gloomy and overwhelmed to enthused and clear. He could see that he knew exactly what to do and how to do it. He also decided to get a PA to help him with the tasks he hated or just wasn't that good at.

He also made a commitment that he would spend at least 1 full day every 2 weeks away from the office, concentrating on strategy, to avoid getting stuck in a rut again.

34 - Using customer feedback to sell more

Customer feedback is a great tool to find out what customers think about you. Not only does it give you valuable information for free, customers like to be asked their opinion, because then they feel more valued. From a practical point of view, you can understand what you are good at and so keep doing it (or get even better at it), whereas negative feedback gives you the opportunity to address genuine problems, which could be losing you business.

Tips

1. **Paper surveys are easy to design** and simple for customers to fill out, but you could use on line surveys or even ring people to find out what they think

2. **Sometimes people don't want to leave their name,** so design the form in a way that makes it clear they don't have to include their contact details if they don't want to

3. **Customer feedback is no good if you don't act on it**. Be committed to making changes if they are required

4. **Say thank you!** Perhaps give customers a discount voucher, or simply ring them to say, 'thank you' for taking the time to fill out the form. This makes them feel valued and more likely to tell you next time if something is not right

5. **Shout about the good things.** Once you know what customers appreciate, include it in your marketing materials, as it will attract more of the same type of people.

Case Study

Hector ran a hardware store with a small team of staff. He had been on some sales training and had learned that customer feedback could be a useful tool to increase sales. Good feedback would help him continue to do the good things and poor feedback would show him the areas he needed to improve, thus improving customer retention and hopefully attracting new customers too.

So, he designed a simple survey, which all the staff gave to customers to fill out and the completed surveys were placed in a sealed box.

After a couple of weeks, he and the staff started to go through the surveys and record the results.

The positives included things like:

- Staff are really helpful
- Easy to find what you want
- Staff have a good knowledge of products
- Always get a friendly welcome
- Good quality products
- Delivery service is fast and reliable
- Early opening and late closing very convenient
- Always answer the phone quickly

The negatives included:

- Not always easy to spot the special offers
- The air conditioning is too cold
- Nowhere to park
- Lighting in the paint section is not very good

He was pleased to see that the positives far outweighed the negatives, but now Hector could take some action too.

Firstly, he got some posters and fliers designed, with the positive comments displayed clearly and the caption "This is what customers say about Hector's Hardware Store". He made sure that one of the posters was displayed prominently in his own shop window and the fliers were handed out to people as they walked past.

Then he started on the negative comments. He got a big notice board, headed it up "Special offers" and made sure that all the deals were displayed on it. He also ordered some new signage for the shop to easily identify the special offers on the individual aisles.

Small Business Sales Dilemmas

He turned down the air conditioning.

He and a couple of his staff spent a morning clearing the overgrown space behind the shop, which was big enough for 2 cars or a small van. They now had parking!

He installed some new spotlights in the paint section which immediately brightened the whole area.

Because he had customers contact details on the survey forms, he now went through them individually, thanking them for taking the time to respond. Where they had given negative feedback, he was able to let them know that he had acted to correct the problems. He sent a 'thank you' card to every single customer who had filled out the survey.

Within a couple of days, the impact was obvious. Footfall was up by about 20% and the customers couldn't wait to tell Hector what they thought about his improvements. Slowly but surely, sales increased. As Hector could track sales by department, he was particularly pleased to notice that more of the special offers were selling and paint sales were up too!

Thereafter, Hector made sure that there was always a pile of survey forms ready to be completed. He regularly checked the feedback and could act fast when required.

35 - Are you leaving persuasive voice mails?

When you cannot get through to a customer or a potential customer, it can be difficult to decide whether to leave a voicemail message.

A long and complicated message may not be listened to by the customer, but by the same token, if they can see that you rang, then good manners would suggest that you say something.

So how can you decide whether to leave a message and, if you do, what should be included?

Tips

1. **Prepare** what you are going to say, in case you cannot get through.

2. **Don't leave a great long message.** Most people simply won't have the patience to listen to it.

3. **Don't keep ringing every 5 minutes** – that's a bit like being a stalker and won't get you a sale!

4. **Keep your message clear** – a mumbled, nervous message with lots of 'ums' and 'ers' will not make you come across in the best possible way.

5. **Keep it relevant** and don't waffle.

Case Study

Ryan had recently qualified as a life coach and was slowly growing his client base. One of his biggest frustrations was that people signed up to his free introductory consultation and then, when he tried to confirm the details of the trial session he couldn't get through to his potential new customers. More often than not, he got voice mail and, unsure of what to say his strategy was to end the call and try again another time.

However, as it became clear that his client base was not growing fast enough, Ryan decided he had to do something, so he set about improving his voice mail messages.

Initially he started with a simple (and rather nervous) "Hi – it's Ryan the Life Coach here. I'm calling to set up your free trial session". That got some response, but when he added a simple "Please call me back to arrange a time that suits you" he noticed an immediate improvement.

Encouraged, he decided to work on improving things further. He did notice that the more he forced himself to leave a message, the more confident he got and that meant his voice sounded more natural on the phone. Realising this, he now started working on sounding positive and enthusiastic and introduced himself with a cheery "Hi – this is Ryan, your friendly local life coach".

He also did some research on the best way to follow up when there was no response. He discovered that it was good to keep trying, but not to overdo it, or he risked becoming a nuisance and making people avoid him. So, he began to organise himself and he started to schedule in some time to ring people. Initially he would call 2 days after they signed up, followed by 3 more calls at 2-day intervals, then weekly and then once a month.

Every time he got voice mail, he left a short, clear and friendly message. However, he also took the trouble to vary his message slightly every time, to avoid being repetitive and to let people know that it was OK if they didn't want him to call any more, but to please let him know so he wasn't turning into a pest.

He was delighted to see that this yielded really good results and that eventually most people booked a firm appointment somewhere between the 2nd and 5th follow up. A few of them took longer, but no one ever told him to stop ringing them!

36 - Are you dressing right for your customers?

When you are selling, it is important to remember that you are a representative of your company – whether it is your own business or you are an employee. If you are a plumber, people would expect you to wear work clothes (but smart, not covered in grease and dirt). If you are selling a professional service of any sort, the safest bet is either a suit or something that is smart/casual. People do make very fast judgements based on the appearance of others, so make sure the first impression you create is a positive one.

Tips

1. **Be smart and professional** – it doesn't matter what you do, if in doubt, err on the side of dressing smarter rather than more casually.

2. **Be appropriate for your work** – in the same way you wouldn't expect to see a fireman wearing a pinstripe suit, make sure your dress code matches your job

3. **Make sure you coordinate** – even if you don't have much money, you can make sure that you are wearing colours and styles that go well together

4. **Don't forget the hygiene** – it might sound obvious, but don't wear clothes that make you sweat – nasty body odours are not going to make you any sales!

5. **Be clean and ironed** – avoid stains, smears and creases to create the best possible impression

Case Study

With a keen interest in science, Shannon had known since school exactly what she wanted to do – create her own line of cosmetics. After graduating, she set about learning everything she could about the industry and, after several years, she finally had her own range ready to bring to market. After all this time, Shannon had pretty much exhausted her funds and so decided to start selling the cosmetics herself until she had enough money to employ someone to do it for her.

She knew exactly who to sell it to, her USPs and the benefits to customers, so, even though she was inexperienced at selling, she was confident she could persuade people to buy. She invested in an online sales training course to help her and off she went.

She created good interest and made a lot of appointments within her target market.

However, she soon realised that she was failing to close any deals. She analysed what she was saying, how she prepared, her samples and the questions she was asking, but she just couldn't come up with a solution.

She found out why by accident.

After a visit to a pharmacist on a rainy day, she went through her usual pitch to no avail and went and sat in her car, wondering what to do. She was just about to drive off, when she realised she had left her umbrella inside. She quickly dashed back into the pharmacy to ask for it.

While Shannon was waiting, she could hear voices – it was the pharmacist and his deputy talking – and they were discussing her! "The products aren't bad are they – but I can't say the same for her! Talk about scruffy". Shannon started to blush. They went on "Do you think she dresses from Oxfam?" There was much muffled laughter. "No, Oxfam wouldn't take that outfit!". At this she made a hasty retreat.

When she got home, she took a long hard look in the mirror. She had been so focussed on developing and selling her cosmetic range that she had completely neglected herself and her appearance. For the first time, she saw a creased blouse, old trousers, comfortable but frankly ugly shoes, one of which was stained. Her hair was a mess and, her cardigan was saggy and had a button missing. She had to accept that, for a representative of a mid – high end line, she didn't look very credible.

Although she didn't have much money left, she made an appointment the very next day with her local department store and asked for the services of a personal shopper to help her put together a work outfit.

The lady listened carefully to find out what Shannon wanted to achieve and came up with a mixture of smart, professional and practical items that could be worn in lots of different combinations. After that, Shannon got a new haircut and, wearing her own cosmetics to perfection, started to make new appointments.

The results were immediate. Impressed by the professional and smart lady in front of them, her prospects turned into paying customers and she finally began to earn some decent money from her cosmetics.

37 - What techniques can you use even if you are inexperienced at selling?

It can be very difficult to sell to customers if you don't have any sort of background or experience in sales. It can feel intimidating and lots of new people in sales roles put themselves under a lot of pressure whilst they learn what is involved.

Fortunately, selling is a lot easier if you are a naturally likeable person and you can focus on what is important to customers. It is also true that just by trying to contact people it is possible to be very successful and sell more than someone with perhaps more skills and knowledge, but who does not physically contact customers.

Tips

1. **Just contact customers** – picking up the phone and having a conversation with them is a great start

2. **Selling is all about building relationships** – so even if you don't know exactly what to say, you can show that you are friendly, reliable and professional

3. **Ask what you can do to help** – after all, if customers have an unresolved issue, you might be able to sort it out and that ensures their satisfaction remains high

4. **Activity is key** – try and contact new people every day – of course some of them won't be interested, but some of them will. By being in the right place at the right time, you will pick up orders

5. **Results aren't always instant** – but by being persistent, they will come

Case Study

After working for several years in an administrative role supporting the sales team, Daniel was asked to apply for a trainee sales role. He got it and was given a vacant territory to manage. He was mentored by Lucas, an experienced and high-performing salesman in the same team.

Although Daniel was keen to get going, he was acutely aware that he didn't have any direct sales experience. He decided he was going to work as hard as possible to hit his targets. He hadn't had any formal training yet, so didn't really have any idea how to structure a sales call, but he was determined to at least try.

He started off by contacting all the existing customers and making appointments with them to introduce himself and find out if they were experiencing any problems or needed help in any way and to make sure they knew about all the current offers and deals.

A few of them placed orders with Daniel, but the majority just chatted and told him about their problems and concerns. Most of them were happy but there were a couple of queries that he could sort out quite easily with his administrative background.

As he reached the end of the month, although he was some way off target, the figures were definitely better than they had been. By the second month, he achieved his target and, by the third month, he got the best result in the team.

Although he was really pleased with this result, he was also worried. He knew that he had still not been on his training and he didn't really know why the figures were so good. He convinced himself that it was just good luck and that the figures would drop again soon.

In fact, he was so concerned that he confided in his mentor, Lucas. He explained that although his figures were good, he didn't really know why and he was worried that the following months would show a drop. Lucas had been on a couple of calls with Daniel and was able to offer some practical reassurance.

He pointed out that Daniel was not 'selling' to customers because he didn't really know about sales yet. However, because of that, ironically, he was taking a genuine interest in trying to help them in the way that he could – in other words by taking the time to visit them, ask about their problems and checking up on whether they knew about special offers. To the customers, this was fantastic – Daniel was providing something more valuable than just selling – he was developing relationships with them and helping them. Lucas explained that actually, this was the real function of selling – to help customers. So, the customers were simply responding by placing orders because Daniel had won their trust and they liked him. His activity and effort in going to see them, combined with his likeability and eagerness to help made a real difference.

Daniel could see that this made sense and, although he wasn't completely convinced, he took Lucas's advice and just kept on doing what he was doing. Sure enough, his figures remained high and improved even more once he completed his training.

38 - Are you asking for the sale enough?

One of the most important skills in selling is being able to close – or ask for the deal. However, even experienced sales people can fail to ask enough times. Statistics show that, on average, even professional sales people tend to ask for the sale about 1.7 times in a sales call or conversation. In other words, if a customer says 'no' the first time they are asked, there is a strong chance that they will not be asked again. This can have drastic results in terms of performance, or for entrepreneurs it can make the difference between getting work and going out of business

Tips

1. **Customers do expect to be asked if they want to go ahead and buy** – so you won't seem pushy if you ask them – it's natural!

2. **There are different closes you can use**, so practice and see which one works best for you.

3. **Don't worry about being word perfect or getting it right** – just ask – remember the more times you ask, the more chance you have of getting the sale

4. **Set yourself a target** to close (say) twice in every conversation with potential customers. As your confidence grows, set a target to close 4 times and then 5.

5. **Measure what works and what doesn't,** so that you know which closes work best for you with your customers.

Case Study

Ellie had decided to sign up for some sales training. She ran her own mobile hairdressing company and desperately wanted to increase sales but realised that with only so many hours in the day, she needed to sell products and extras to generate more income. However, she didn't know where to start.

She found a course which covered, amongst other things, how to close. She learned that most people do not ask for the sale (or close) nearly enough times, even though customers are often ready to buy. She also learned about 5 main closing techniques that she could use in her own business:

Trial close

This is a way of checking to see if the customer is ready to sign or buy. You ask the question and then WAIT! Watch and listen carefully for their response. If they are not sure yet, or come up with a reason why they don't want to go ahead, then take time to address their concerns. Then you can try closing again.

Examples:
- How does that sound to you?
- Does that meet your requirements?

Direct close

This is simply asking the customer for their business. It is very straightforward to use, but can feel as though it is a bit pushy. There is also the risk that they might just say 'no', which can make you feel a bit stuck about what to do next. However, the advantage of this close is that it does get straight to the point.

Examples:
- Do you want to go ahead?
- Shall we proceed with the order?
- May I count on your business?

Assumptive Close

This is when you 'assume' the customer is ready to buy, so instead of asking them directly if they want to go ahead, you focus on some of the details instead. This makes it a lot softer than a direct close.

Examples:
- When shall we deliver it?
- Will 20 cases be enough?
- Are you paying for that by card?

Alternative Close

This is another softer type of close because here you are giving the customer a choice of detail instead of directly asking if they want to go ahead.

Examples:
- Would you prefer the red or the blue?
- Do you want the small or the medium size?
- Do you prefer Option A or Option B?

Conditional Close

When a customer gives you an objection, perhaps after you have tried closing using one of the techniques above, then a conditional close can be a great way to get the sale. They always start with 'If I……' and basically you are trying to make a deal with them, to gain their commitment.

Examples:
- If I ring the factory and they have a red one, will you go ahead today?
- If I can train all your staff, will you take this package?
- If I can get you finance, will you choose the premium version?

With the help of these 5 closes, Ellie had a structure she could follow. After a bit of trial and error, she worked out that in her business, if she used the trial close, followed by the alternative close, most of the time she managed to sell extra products. After 6 months, she was generating about 35% more business, just by applying this simple technique.

39 - How to make sure you are not using language that makes customers avoid you

There are certain words and phrases that are considered clichés in the world of selling. If you want to avoid looking like an insincere salesperson, or one who is just following a script, then it is a good idea not to fall into the trap of using tired, unimaginative words and phrases. That doesn't mean that you need to have the vocabulary of Shakespeare, but you should at least try to say things in your own way.

Tips

1. **Don't use clichés** – instead use your own words

2. **Listen to yourself** – if you can, record some of your calls – you will notice all sorts of things that you didn't realise you were doing and then you can work on eliminating bad habits

3. **Never start a call with "How are you?"** It absolutely screams "You're trying to sell me something"

4. **Always remember you are talking to a real person** – for all you know they could have had 20 other people calling them today trying to sell to them. So, put yourself in their shoes

5. **If you sound insincere, then as far as the customer is concerned, you probably are insincere.** Work hard to show that you are genuine

Case Study

Edwin was new to sales and he was determined to do well. He had been out with his boss during his training and now he was starting to go on visits by himself. He was bursting with enthusiasm, loved the products – which were advanced water treatment systems - and he really enjoyed going out and meeting new customers.

He started to close sales, but soon realised that selling was not always as easy as his boss had made it look. He really struggled with some of the seasoned and experienced buyers that he had to approach to stock his product.

One, refused to give Edwin an appointment. He tried every week to arrange a visit, but the buyer just wasn't having any of it. In frustration, Edwin asked his boss if he could listen in to his phone conversation to see if there was something he was missing. In fact, his boss went one step further – he recorded the call. When Edwin asked for feedback, his boss told him to listen to the call and see if he could work it out.

Edwin was horrified. He heard himself using what seemed like every cliché in the book. "How are you today", "To be honest", "Quite Frankly". It was as though he had suddenly lost the power to speak in English!

His boss kindly explained that the buyer didn't want to talk to an automaton who only spoke in trite sales terms; rather he wanted to talk to a real human being who cared about what was important to him. He also pointed out that by using phrases like "Frankly" and "To be honest" he was coming across as insincere and was giving the impression that he was either hiding something, or worse, lying.

By asking "How are you today?" Edwin was coming over particularly insincerely – as his boss pointed out, his job was to sell, the buyer knew his job was to sell and, apart from wasting time it was probably actually annoying the buyer and eroding confidence in Edwin's product. He explained, the moment you hear someone say that on the phone, you know they don't care and that they are trying to appear polite, but couldn't care less how you are – they just want to sell you something.

Edwin's boss gave him some other pointers too – for example making sure he was never rude or disrespectful to the competition, never starting a conversation by asking if the buyer wanted to place an order and to just use his own authentic and real words.

With his boss standing by him, Edwin rang his elusive buyer again. When he got through, he apologised for his previous call, saying he was new. He used his own language, explained that he thought he had something the buyer might be interested in seeing and politely asked for an appointment. The buyer said 'yes', on the condition that Edwin did not use the word "Honestly". Edwin unreservedly agreed.

40 - Do you proactively seek out your customers' pain points?

Although on the face of it, seeking pain points might seem negative, it is one of the most valuable things you can do for a customer. If you can genuinely understand what causes them the biggest pain and then solve it for them, you will not only sell more but you will tangibly help them in one of the best possible ways. Although customers do buy because something is nice to have, they will be much more likely to buy if you can solve a real and pressing worry or fear.

Tips

1. **Most business owners have the same concerns and worries** – make money, save money, save time and avoid effort, so work out what you can do to help with these

2. **Don't tell people what you do** – tell them what you achieve for them

3. **Be very specific about how you help customers** – use facts, statistics and benefits rather than vague terms.

4. **Use language that your clients will understand** – keep it simple and avoid jargon

5. **If you are not sure exactly what you do to remove clients' fears and pain, then ask them** – do a survey or ask if you can interview them to find out

Case Study

Dan had been a professional business coach for many years with a national organisation. He decided to set up on his own, because he was frustrated with his inability to influence his own income.

After careful planning, he started marketing his new business. He did lots of things that came under the umbrella of business coaching, for example:

- Business plans
- Team building
- Vision and Mission statements
- Strategising
- Setting business goals
- Time Management

He made sure that his website and literature reflected this and he also went networking to promote his business. He was realistic and knew that it would probably take a while to fill his practice, but he was frustrated that progress seemed to be extremely slow.

He made sure that every time he met a potential customer, he listed all his skills, in case one of them was the thing that the customer needed, but people just didn't seem that interested in him.

However, by chance, he found out what he was doing wrong.

At a networking event, he bumped into an old client that he used to work with in his previous job. The client was delighted to see Dan and chatted enthusiastically with him. She couldn't wait to tell him all the things she had achieved because of working with him and how much her business had grown.

When the meeting started, everyone took turns to talk for one minute about their business. Dan's ex-client said her piece and then added that she wanted to give a testimonial about Dan.

She explained how Dan had come along when she was absolutely overwhelmed with work, to the extent that she was hardly seeing her family, she was on prescription drugs and was on the verge of giving up her business. Thanks to Dan's ability to help her get clear on what she needed, she started to delegate, restrategise and begin to work 'on' her business instead of 'in' it. She finished by saying that her turnover had gone up by 60% in the past year and it was thanks to Dan that she had got her work/life balance back and was absolutely loving her business now. She told the audience "If you have fallen out of love with your business, you need Dan – he's a business fixer."

Dan was of course, delighted to hear this and thanked her. However, what he hadn't expected was the reaction among the other networkers. One by one, a steady stream of people came over to him to ask what exactly he did. He explained how he got results with clients by fixing their areas of pain and worry and by helping them do the big stuff like earn more, reduce stress, improve work/life balance and get their motivation back.

The penny really dropped when one regular networker said to him "I had no idea you did all that – I thought you were some sort of administrator."

After the meeting, Dan sat down to rework his networking pitch and to amend all his marketing materials. He started to think about what problems he solved for his desperate clients and how he helped them overcome their worst fears and issues. Once he did this, he immediately noticed an improvement in enquiries – it seemed that customers didn't care what he did, just how he helped them.

41 - Are you falling into the discounting trap?

It is vital not to get into the habit of discounting too frequently and thereby eroding your profit margins. If you give a discount too quickly, there is a risk that the customer will think the product or service was overpriced in the first place or they may be tempted to try and get an even bigger discount. Of course, there is always the possibility that if you undercut a competitor, they will then undercut you and you both end up in a price war – that way no one wins.

Tips

1. **Work out your profit margins** – then make sure you do not drop below a certain point

2. **Find out what the market charges** – some of your competitors will probably charge more and some less. Work out where you sit within the range.

3. **Choose a price and stick to it** – tell customers you don't discount, but you do sometimes have special offers (then you can encourage them to go on your marketing list)

4. **Be confident** – some people will always buy even if you don't give a discount. These are your ideal customers so you really want more of them!

5. **Try and add value** – if you can ensure that customers are getting more for their money, they are less likely to ask for a discount.

Case Study

The philosophy behind Esme's Craft Emporium was that customers would have access to genuine, handmade, unique quality items. Esme made all her products herself – she specialised in crafts for the home. She sold them at craft fairs and school fetes in the summer, or seasonal events, like Christmas fairs then spent the quiet months making more.

Small Business Sales Dilemmas

She absolutely loved what she did and got immense satisfaction from seeing her items sold to people who clearly loved them and appreciated the effort that had gone into making them. However, she had noticed that, although her costs had increased, her sales had dropped. She was busy, but she couldn't work out exactly what was happening.

She found out by chance. She was exhibiting at a Christmas fair and her stand was next to a lady who sold hats and scarves. As was common at these events, the two exhibitors chatted with one another and covered for each other when one needed a break.

On the second day, Esme was at lunch. On her return, she saw her neighbour selling some cushion covers to a lady, so she rushed over to help. The customer loved the cushion covers and was trying to work out how many to buy. She asked Esme if she could have a discount if she bought 4. Esme agreed, delighted – the sale was worth about £80, so she could discount by about £20 she reckoned and still have £60 profit.

The sale complete, Esme thanked her neighbour for helping. To her surprise, the lady turned around to her and said, "why did you discount?" Esme explained that she would still make £60 profit from selling the 4 cushion covers.

Shaking her head, the neighbour asked how long it took to make something like the cushion covers and how much the materials cost. Esme said it took about 45 minutes each and the cost of the materials was about £10 per cushion cover.

"My dear, I've been next to you for a full day now, and I hope you don't mind me saying, but you must stop discounting. The materials cost £40 and the labour took 3 hours. I don't know what you pay yourself, but £20 for 3 hours work doesn't seem like much – and then deduct whatever you paid for this stand. You are selling at a loss – and that customer would have paid the full price with no problem."

Esme immediately started to argue, but suddenly she wondered if the woman was right – it would explain her drop in income. Seeing her confusion, the woman suggested that Esme could just try saying 'no' next time someone asked for a discount, to see how it went.

Sure enough, the very next customer did ask for a discount, but Esme held firm – and got the sale anyway. At the end of the day, she calculated that 9 further customers had asked for a discount. All except one had bought at the asking price, ensuring that Esme made decent margins on everything. Even though her immediate reaction was to discount to get the sale, she could see that she must hold firm and customers would still buy anyway.

42 - How can you keep sales strong at seasonally quiet times of the year?

It is undeniable that certain businesses can have seasonal peaks and troughs – for example, while many businesses thrive at Christmas, for others it is a very slow time, when many people do not seem to have disposable income or the time to make any purchases except Christmas presents.

This can cause problems, but it is important not to use the time of year as an excuse – after all, as a small business owner you still need to eat and pay your bills.

Tips

1. **Don't convince yourself that people won't buy during a certain period** – there is always someone who needs what you have

2. **Don't accept "I can't afford it now"** – if you had an emergency like a punctured tyre or a parking ticket you had to pay before it doubled in cost, then the chances are you would find the money somehow. Customers are the same.

3. **If people won't buy now, do the next best thing and make an appointment instead.** That way you can ensure that you have lots of business meetings in January

4. **Christmas can be an opportunity** – if an urgent need crops up and no one else is open, then they might use you – just make sure they know how to reach you.

5. **Be cheerful** – there is a lot of goodwill around at Christmas so make the most of it and get those meetings that you couldn't get at other times of the year.

Case Study

George hated the Christmas period. He ran a stationery company and Christmas was always such a slow period for him. He often just closed the offices for the entire week between Christmas and New Year, because most of his customers were on holiday too.

However, he had just employed a new salesman – Keith – who was really enthusiastic about, well, everything really.

What George didn't know was that Keith had a massive mortgage and a first child on the way. He was therefore trying to earn every penny that he could. The thought of just stopping for a whole week was inconceivable – Keith wanted to build up the customer orders now – he could always take holidays later.

So, Keith didn't follow accepted wisdom and slow down as Christmas approached – he just carried on prospecting. Yes, it was harder to get people on the phone and hardly anyone returned his calls, but he just kept plugging away. He had worked out that if he could persuade people to place an order over Christmas, then he could sell the benefit of having all the stationery in place, thus ensuring that businesses could 'hit the ground running' in January.

He also decided he was going to be super-positive (after all, it was Christmas!) and, where he couldn't get an actual order, just book in an appointment with his customers for the earliest possible date in January.

He had mixed results, but George had to admit that Keith was doing very well. He got 3 customers to place quite significant orders just before Christmas and he had a diary full of appointments for the first 2 weeks of January. Keith had asked if he could continue to work over the Christmas and New Year week and George gave him permission to do so, on the understanding that George would have to be there if any orders needed to be fulfilled.

It was during this week that Keith had his best result. He was in the process of calling customers, as usual, when he got through to an office manager at a local copy shop. She was not very happy about working during the Christmas break and she and Keith had a long chat about all sorts of things – except, ironically, work. At the end of the conversation, she admitted that it had been good to have someone to talk to at such a quiet time. She told Keith how let down and disappointed she had been by the behaviour of her current stationery supplier. She asked about the products, turnaround and prices, which Keith could answer. She took his number and said she was going to think about what she needed.

4 hours later, she emailed over an order worth 30% of Keith's monthly target. Keith immediately rang George, so that the order could be fulfilled on time. George genuinely thought Keith was joking when he gave him the total figure. But he soon realised he wasn't!

Later, in January when George was going through the figures, he realised that Keith had generated more business that December than in any year since the company had started. He was happy to have his preconceptions proved wrong.

43 - Are you making the most of the Competitive Advantage of being a small business?

As a small business, you are probably very aware of your larger competitors and it can be very easy to be intimidated by them. The trick is not to fall into the trap of trying to match them. If you go head to head with them, the chances are that they will win, so you need to be smart. Much like the Bible story of David and Goliath, if you match your strengths to their weaknesses, then you can consistently beat them.

Tips

1. **Small businesses are often more flexible** – so if there is a new trend you can capitalise on it immediately, whereas a big company would have to do research and get it approved by many levels internally

2. **You can do things faster** – you are a speedboat to a big corporation's ocean liner, so that means you can make changes at a moment's notice

3. **Build better relationships with customers** – with a small business each customer really matters and the chances are that they will prefer dealing with a real person rather than an automated system

4. **Use the local community** – as a small local business you have an immediate advantage with other local businesses

5. **It is easier to manage your costs** – after all you don't have to pay for a Head Office!

Case Study

Sasha had decided to set up a business offering a corporate gift service. She had worked in retail for many years and understood how to source products and had a huge list of contacts to help her.

Initially she decided to focus on medium-sized businesses because she thought they would be the sort of customers who would appreciate her bespoke, highly personalised service. She was also conscious that, as her business was still a start-up, she might have to explain her lack of a track record and thought that smaller, newer businesses might be more understanding.

Business was slow, but it was improving. However, one day a contact said she thought a buyer in a large finance house would be really interested in seeing her. Sasha refused, saying she was not ready and that they would probably try and force her to discount.

Fortunately for Sasha, her contact persisted and eventually persuaded her to have a meeting with the buyer.

The buyer couldn't have been more welcoming. It turned out that they preferred to deal with smaller businesses. Sasha asked why.

The buyer explained that when they wanted to provide corporate gifts, they liked bespoke, high end, unique items. Larger organisations couldn't guarantee that level of attention to detail. He also said that they sometimes needed a fast delivery, or needed to change the specification at short notice. Overall, smaller companies were much more responsive and able to accommodate them, helped hugely by the fact that, in his experience, it was a lot easier to get through to a decision-maker. From his perspective as a busy buyer, it just made the whole process a lot easier, which meant he was happier too.

They turned to a discussion of the products Sasha could offer. The buyer was very keen to see samples of the kinds of bespoke gifts that were possible. At the end of the meeting, the buyer asked how quickly Sasha could deliver an order of 60 items. Satisfied with her answer, he confirmed that he would like to go ahead and order them. To Sasha's amazement, he accepted the price without pressurising her to reduce it and they shook hands on the spot.

That was the beginning of a long and successful relationship – Sasha's company was a perfect fit for the finance house and she in turn, soon discovered that they were the ideal customer for her.

44 - Are you trying to sell when you shouldn't be?

When you are very passionate about what you do, it can be tempting to tell everyone about it, but that can be a problem, because you can come across as pushy and only interested in your own business. Instead, particularly if you use marketing strategies such as networking, then you need to do the basics first, which in sales, is all about finding out about your customer first. People or businesses will only ever buy from organisations they trust and like, so if you get them to talk about themselves rather than what you have to offer, then you are much more likely to build long-term business relationships with them.

Tips

1. **No one likes being 'sold to'** – so don't jump straight in with a sales pitch

2. **Take time to find out about your potential customer** – good selling is about building relationships, so ask them questions and show a genuine interest in what they say

3. **It is quite unlikely that a customer will buy from you the first time they meet you** – so accept that sometimes a sale is a slow burn – maybe they will use you in a week, or a month or a year.

4. **People buy from people** – so even if you have the best product or service in the world, no one will buy from you if they don't like you. Try to do simple things like smiling and being friendly.

5. **Show an interest in other people** – if you are networking, listen attentively and respectfully to others, just as you hope they would do when it is your turn

Small Business Sales Dilemmas

Case Study

Eric had just joined a networking group. His business was telecoms and he could provide most customers with a cheaper rate than other suppliers, so he knew that he had the potential to do very well. He also knew that networking could be a great way of meeting and influencing people so he had done his research and joined a local group.

Prior to his first meeting he got everything ready – business cards, brochures, sign-up forms and a one-minute sales pitch to really get people excited about his service.

He arrived and the host welcomed him. She explained how the meeting worked and introduced him to a few other networkers. Delighted, he wasted no time in introducing himself and his service to the other people. He was pleased that he had spoken to 6 people before the meeting began properly.

During this part of the meeting, everyone spent one-minute explaining who they were and what they did. Eric was pleased to hear that there was loads of potential for him to sell his telecoms services to them. When it came to his turn, he wasted no time. He explained enthusiastically how good his company was, how good the service was, how cheap they were and how everyone would pretty much be silly not to sign up straight away.

He sat down, satisfied that he had done a good job and that he would make some sales that day. He sat through the rest of the meeting, including a 15-minute talk from one of the other members, but really all he was waiting for was to talk to more people at the end and get some sign-ups.

At the end, he began to circulate. However, to his surprise, he couldn't seem to get anyone to engage with him properly – all they seemed to be interested in was finding out a bit more about him – not his amazing telecoms service. He didn't sign up a single person.

The next week, he got there even earlier for the meeting, to make sure he caught as many people as possible. Although plenty of the members spoke to him, no one wanted to talk about signing up with him. He couldn't understand it. He put even more effort into his one-minute pitch, urging people to sign up straight away for maximum discounts.

At the end of the meeting, he noticed the network leader beckon to him. She took him to one side and asked how it was going. Eric took the opportunity to let her know that he was finding it very frustrating – no one had bought from him yet.

The network leader sympathised and asked Eric if he had ever been networking before. Eric admitted he hadn't. She invited him to sit down and explained kindly that networking was about building relationships. "Once people know you, they will hopefully like and trust you – then they will consider doing business with you". She told Eric that he had gone in too hard and too fast – trying to sell without doing the basics of getting to know fellow members. She suggested that next time he just concentrated on asking people about themselves. "If you just try and sell to them, they will switch off, but if you show a genuine interest in them, then you will start to build relationships. Try it and see!" She also pointed out that if he just tried to sell, then people would probably start to avoid him; instead she encouraged him to aim to set some appointments.

Although it seemed completely counter-intuitive to Eric, he gave it a go and, the following week, although he didn't get any sales, he did arrange 3 meetings. From then on, he spent more time finding out about people and less time selling, which ironically, meant he sold more!

45 - Do your customers consider you a credible option?

Customers often make buying decisions without even realising why. However, first impressions count for a lot and it is important that the image of your business says the right things about you. For example, you should make sure your message is consistent and professional. You don't need to spend a fortune, but sometimes using a professional to help you can be a good investment, leaving you to focus on the things you are good at.

Tips

1. **Check your website regularly and look at it as though you were a potential customer** – in other words, is it easy to navigate around, up-to-date and does it provide relevant and useful information?

2. **Is your branding consistent** – check your logo, colours and tag lines are the same across your leaflets, website, cards and any other promotional material

3. **Ask someone you trust to give you honest feedback** – it doesn't have to be a paid professional – a fellow business colleague or friend should be able to tell you what their first impression is and then if necessary you can change the things that don't work so well

4. **Check out what your best competitors do** – see what works well, what you like the look of and what ideas you can adapt to suit your own business – this is not about copying, rather learning from more experienced and successful businesses and applying it to your own

5. **Ask your existing customers why they chose you** – then make sure that your publicity material reflects this. You should also make sure this is something you mention to potential customers – after all, if it brought them to you, then it will probably bring others too

Case Study

When Caren heard about a free seminar for start-ups in her local area she signed up immediately. She had been trading for 9 months as a mobile health and beauty therapist but had failed to achieve the growth she so desperately needed. She hoped the seminar would tell her what she was doing wrong so that she could change things.

The seminar was delivered by a sales and marketing expert and right from the beginning, the focus was on credibility. Caren had always believed that by providing a good service and working hard, she would get business through happy customers referring her and through repeat business, but she soon learned that she was making some very basic mistakes that could be preventing her from getting leads and worse, preventing her from making sales. The speaker explained how potential customers make judgements based on the overall feel of a company and by getting even one thing a bit wrong, it affects your credibility and therefore can put people off using you.

As soon as the seminar was over, she returned home and got to work. This is what she changed:

1. She bought a domain name for her website and made sure her email had the same name. This was more professional than the mismatching and generic emails she had had before

2. She made sure she started answering the phone by giving a cheerful greeting, stating the company name and asking, "How can I help?" Before she had just said "Hello" which meant she missed an opportunity to create a great first impression.

3. She rang up 4 of her most regular customers and asked them if they would give her a written recommendation that she could put on her website. They all agreed willingly. Caren now knew how important it was to have happy testimonials from customer to demonstrate her trustworthiness

4. She published a clear list of prices and put them on the website. Previously she had given the prices verbally, which meant that a lot of customers tried to negotiate the price. By putting things in writing, she knew she would now get less price objections

5. She asked a graphic designer to create a new leaflet for her – it

didn't cost much but she was able to put her new prices, her new website address and new email on it. It meant that her branding was now more consistent and she had something to give to both existing customers and potential customers. She also got her business cards updated at the same time

Straight away, Caren started to feel a new kind of confidence – she had always been proud of her business, but now she felt it even more. With her new professional touches, she knew she was giving a much better impression to her customers and she was getting lots of positive comments. She also began to get new enquiries – many more than before and, with her new-found self-belief realised that she was enjoying talking with customers. As many of them had already seen the leaflets or visited the website, all she had to do was tell them about the details and the results they could expect – in fact, the bit she enjoyed the most! She noticed her sales steadily increase and it hadn't even been that hard.

46 - Can adversity help you sell more effectively?

There are lots of things that can go wrong in a business and which can cause genuine disruption. However, sometimes problems and challenges can reveal a better way of doing things, or force business owners to rethink things and maybe come up with something new and productive.

It is also true, that sometimes when the pressure is highest that people can work the hardest to bring in sales – a trend that any manager of a sales team will recognise – as when most of the sales come in during the last few days before cut-off for the month or year.

Tips

1. **If a business problem occurs, then try and find an alternative way of doing things** – it might not be the most obvious thing to do, in fact, it could be completely different, but try and think of a way around it

2. **A problem shared is a problem halved** – in other words, ask other people to come up with suggestions. Even if you don't ultimately use their ideas, most people appreciate being asked, which can be great for staff morale

3. **Don't overthink things** – sometimes it can be best just to try something, even if you are not quite sure whether it will work or not. Some of the best things have been discovered by accident!

4. **When marketing, potential customers respond better to various methods of contact (or touches)** – so vary your methods and use a mixture of email, direct mail, telephone, social media, face-to-face and any other methods you think are appropriate

5. **Necessity is the mother of invention** – if you really, really have to find a solution, then you probably will! Look upon problems as opportunities to become even better.

Case Study

Zac worked with his friend and business partner Clifford in a software company. Clifford was the technical person, whereas Zac's job was to market and sell the software to small businesses. He was very good at what he did and used the latest technology to help generate leads and grow them into paying customers.

Clifford was due to go away on a short trip and he and Zac went through the usual check list of things before Clifford left the office for the last time. There had been a few problems with the automated system Zac used to develop leads and Clifford said that he had sorted it out with the service provider, so Zac was not unduly worried.

However, the next day when Zac came to work, he realised that the system was not functioning at all. He couldn't reach Clifford, who was probably on a plane and Zac realised he didn't know who to contact. Neither did the junior staff. After spending a frustrating hour trying to work it out and failing, Zac was interrupted by the juniors, who told him that they had finished all their current work and wanted to know what to do next.

There was nothing else scheduled so Zac told them to check the emails and see if any new orders had been placed. There were none.

Zac was stuck – he didn't want to pay his staff to just sit around, but with the automated system not working, it was quite likely that no new orders were going to come in.

In desperation, he told the two juniors to print off a list of prospects who had expressed an interest in their software and he told them they were going to do some telephoning.

While they were doing that, he used his knowledge of sales to create a list of questions the juniors could ask prospective customers. When they returned he explained that they were to work through the list and when they got through to the contact, they were to ask the questions on the list and write down the answers. The questions were not pushy, rather they were things like 'what did you think of the video we sent you?", "when were you thinking of purchasing?", "what sort of things are important to you when you are making a purchase like this?" and "is there anything you would like to ask me or anything you don't understand?"

They worked at this all day and had some very interesting results. Overall, most of the people they got through to were very pleased to have received a phone call, because they had never had anything except an automated email.

They were also very happy to answer the questions, giving Zac loads of useful information about when to call customers back, several requests for a visit and a couple of people who said they had meant to order but had just forgotten. It was a very productive day. Zac realised that he had neglected the telephone as a means of contacting customers and had been relying exclusively on email technology. He decided to continue the phoning the next day and build in one day a week exclusively to calling potential customers.

When Clifford finally got Zac's message, he left a voicemail telling Zac what to do. That meant that Zac could sort out the automated system, which he did, but he was determined never to rely on just one system ever again.

47 - Are you prejudging your customers?

Many people have certain preconceptions of what their ideal customers look or behave like. Whist there will be times when this is a good guideline, there will always be exceptions to the rule and it is sensible not to make too many prejudgements about people.

To illustrate the point, think about the famous scene in the film Pretty Woman, where Julia Roberts' character tries to spend loads of money and the shop assistant won't take her money.

Tips

1. **Just because a person looks affluent, it doesn't mean they are** – it might all be borrowed and they are drowning in debt. Similarly, someone who dresses scruffily might be wealthy

2. **Sometimes the simplest, least fussy people can be the best customers** – it is the ones who put on a show that can be difficult

3. **Take time to find out, through good questioning, exactly what the customer wants** – if you make assumptions you might miss something amazing

4. **Don't jump to conclusions** – sometimes you need to hear a person's story to gain context

5. **Treat everyone as though they are important** – because when you are a customer, that's how you want to be treated

Case Study

Warren ran a busy car dealership on the outskirts of a major city. Trade was brisk and his team of 4 salespeople served a wide variety of customers.

Warren's office overlooked the main showroom and one day, as he sat doing paperwork, he noticed a blind customer with her guide dog in the salesroom. He wasn't sure if she was with anyone and glanced around to see if she was being helped. She was standing quietly by the entrance and after about 10 minutes, none of his staff had approached her, so Warren decided to go himself.

He introduced himself warmly and asked if he could help the lady. She explained that she wanted to buy a car. Warren wasn't quite sure if she really meant it and, rather expecting to be told she was pulling his leg, he dug a little deeper.

It turned out that, although she was indeed blind, she was in the market for a new car and she wanted a big one because of her dog. She had a driver arranged – her son lived with her and he would be driving it. Not only that, she was very well informed and knew exactly what sort of features she wanted and had a good idea of the technical specifications too.

Warren organised some test drives for her, discussed different options, including some alternative finance arrangements and asked her whether she would like to go ahead. In fact, because she was very likeable and had obviously done her homework, she was extremely easy to deal with.

The lady not only went ahead and made a purchase from him, but she chose a top of the range model with lots of extras. Warren made very good commission on the car. Even better, because she was so happy with the customer service Warren had provided, she recommended 2 of her friends to Warren as well, meaning he got 2 more very lucrative sales within just a few weeks. In fact, over the next few years, this customer returned again and again every time she wanted to upgrade.

Although Warren was delighted with his sale, he was also sobered, because he realised that his staff had been wrong to ignore this lady – they had made a judgment that a blind person could not possibly be in the market for a car. He had to take responsibility for their preconceptions and decided to raise it as a specific training issue.

At the next staff meeting he went through the figures and explained how any one of them could have earned a lot of very easy commission from a charming customer, if only they had not pre-judged her. He made sure all the staff made a point of welcoming anyone from that moment on … after all, even the most unlikely looking people could be genuine customers.

48 - Are you losing sales because you are not taking care of the little things?

Everyone makes judgements about others and that includes customers, who may make up their mind about who to buy from based on all sorts of different factors. No matter how brilliant the product, friendly the person selling it, or established-looking the company is, little things can put customers off from purchasing.

A good example is where you don't do something simple that you are supposed to and the customer just loses faith in you. It spoils their overall impression of your organisation and can be hard to win back their trust.

Tips

1. **A lot of customers make a buying decision based on the details** – so don't be tempted to ignore them

2. **Remember that every contact you have with the customer can influence them** – it could be visual, verbal, written or just a feeling, but stay professional always

3. **It is better to do something imperfectly than not at all** – in other words, if you don't have a perfect letter and you wait until you do, probably nothing will ever happen.

4. **If you can't do something for a genuine reason, say so** – it is important to keep communicating with customers so that they know why a delay has occurred.

5. **A chain is only as strong as the weakest link** – so just because you are amazing at the main thing you do, you mustn't expect it to get you out of trouble if the bad things are really bad!

Case Study

Jimmy was an animal portrait painter and was very good at it. He got most of his business through referrals, but had decided to start trying out other ways of promoting his business and booked a stand at a county craft fair.

His paintings were a true labour of love and he always went the extra mile to make sure that he truly captured the personality of the pet and that the owner was delighted with the final results. He would spend whatever time and effort was needed to do sketches, plans, colouring or framing, but to him it was not a chore, just part of the whole wonderful process.

However, when it came to paperwork and administration, he was not so thorough – he just didn't enjoy it and did the bare minimum so that he could do what he loved – painting.

At the county fair, he displayed as many portraits as possible and got a good amount of interest. A few people even booked him to come and visit for preliminary sketches, which he was very pleased with. A far greater number left their details so that he could get in touch with them later.

Jimmy didn't much like writing – preferring to speak with potential customers instead, so over the next few weeks, he began to call them. Some people wanted to find out more and 3 of them asked for a quote in writing.

Jimmy put off doing it. He didn't have a clue what to write in a quote, so rather than find out, he did a bit of painting. About a week later, one of his contacts rang up to find out where the quote was. He made an excuse and promised to do it. Of course, he didn't. They called again a few days later, explaining that they just needed something in writing – it didn't need to be fancy, but could Jimmy please do it.

Finally, Jimmy found a sample of a quotation on line and used that to structure his letter. He emailed it over and within 30 minutes he received a confirmation email that the customer wanted to go ahead. He couldn't believe it had been so easy.

Straight away, he contacted the other 2 prospects who had asked for quotes, to say sorry for taking so long. However, this time the reaction was a bit different. The first person he rang was a lady who had absolutely loved his canine portraits and had 4 dogs of her own. When she heard it was Jimmy, she explained that although she had really wanted to use him, another portrait painter had approached her and had been able to give her a price straight away. Because he had been so fast and was also very good, she had engaged him and he was right in the middle of the commission at that time.

The second contact was much blunter. "I wanted to use you, but you couldn't even make the effort to send me a price – that was 3 weeks ago. If it takes that long to do a bit of paperwork, how long will it take to do a painting? I've changed my mind."

Once the reality had set in that Jimmy had lost 2 lucrative pieces of work just because he had been slow to send in a simple quote, he decided on a strict policy of quoting within 48 hours. There were plenty of reasons why a client might choose not to use him, but he was going to make sure that being bad at administration was not going to be one of them.

49 - Are you trying too hard and offering too much?

When you are with a potential customer and they want something, it can be very tempting to just say 'yes' – after all, you want to show that you can deliver, that you are capable and that you are helpful. However, it can become a slippery slope because the customer may make more and more requests. Each time you say 'yes' to something that is not reasonable or part of your core package, it can erode your profitability and worse, if you can't deliver, it can affect your levels of customer service and ultimately, your ability to deliver on your promises.

Tips

1. **Only say 'yes' to things that are already part of your normal package** – unless you can charge extra for them

2. **Ask why** – sometimes customers just ask for things because they want them, not because they need them. If you ask them why, you can uncover the real reasons

3. **Be assertive** – if you are confident in your main package and the value that it delivers, then you will not feel the need to say yes to things when people ask

4. **Keep an eye on the profits** – if you can give something to a customer which is of value to them, but does not cost you much, then it might be worth going ahead

5. **Don't be afraid to walk away** – if the customer is asking too much, then they might not be a good fit for you anyway

Case Study

Gwyneth was a graphic designer and had just started out on her own after many years of working with a large organisation.

She didn't have very many clients, so was keen to get as many new ones as possible. When an enquiry came in from an academic institution who wanted to produce new prospectuses and marketing materials for the next academic year, it was just the sort of job that Gwyneth really wanted.

Her contact gave her a very clear specification and Gwyneth made an appointment to go and see her and discuss in more detail what was required. During the meeting, lots of questions were asked about how much experience Gwyneth had and the buyer made it quite clear that she had doubts about whether the work would be up to the required standard. Under pressure, Gwyneth began to worry that she wouldn't get the work. When the buyer asked if she would be available outside of normal office hours, Gwyneth said 'yes – of course'. The buyer seemed reassured, but then asked about how many proofs would be provided. Normally it was 2, but Gwyneth said, 'as many as you need'. And so, it went on – the buyer asking for more things on top of the specification and Gwyneth saying 'yes' for fear she would not be chosen.

However, a few days later, she got the confirmation that she had won the work, together with a contract which included all the extras she had promised.

What should have been a pleasurable job turned out to be one of the worst projects Gwyneth had ever taken on. Accountable inside and outside of working hours, making change after change to tight deadlines, the pressure started to build. The work began to take over her entire practice, leaving her no time to get new clients and neglecting the few she did have.

Eventually, the project was completed on time, but after going through the figures, Gwyneth realised that she had made hardly any profit, because of the amount of extra time and effort she had expended. The client was really pleased with the work, but Gwyneth already knew that she didn't want to repeat the experience again.

Instead, she drew up a list of items that clients could have, but which would incur an additional cost – that way, if they asked, they could make the decision about whether it was worth it or not and she would not be out of pocket. Most of all, she vowed never to just say 'yes' to win another job, unless the customer was asking for something she already provided.

50 - How do you know if you are getting 'out there' enough?

It can be very tempting to throw money at marketing and then to just sit back and wait for the orders to come in. However, without having a system of active prospecting, this strategy may result in very few enquiries and, even worse, very few paying customers.

Instead, as part of your overall sales and marketing strategy, it is important to proactively seek new customers. These will be the customers who might not see your advertisements, brochures or websites, so provide a totally different revenue stream.

Tips

1. **Sales do not happen by magic** – selling to customers always requires some sort of effort, so be prepared to be proactive

2. **Be consistent** – do something every day wherever possible, because that ensures your activity levels are constant.

3. **Active prospecting means you will get customers that your competitors won't** – so for example, if they are just relying on advertising and you are not, you will have access to the customers who don't see your competitors' adverts.

4. **Don't worry about your skill level** – it is better to do something (even if it isn't perfect) than nothing while you wait to become perfect

5. **Try different ways of contacting customers** – you will find that some work better than others. When you work out which work best, you can concentrate your effort on this area.

Small Business Sales Dilemmas

Case Study

Leonora had just started her own business providing HR consultancy to small and medium sized businesses. She had many years' experience in the area, having worked for a large company doing the same type of thing.

Now as a start-up herself, Leonora knew she needed to get her name out there so she invested some money in advertising and marketing and began to wait for the enquiries to come in. She didn't get the flood she had expected.

In the first month, she only got 2 enquiries and neither of them ended up using her. By the time she lost her third enquiry, she was going crazy with worry. In desperation, she rang a friend who managed a team of salespeople and asked what she should do.

The friend asked her questions about how many visits she went on, how many phone calls she made, how many prospecting letters she sent out and how much she engaged with people on social media. Apart from the one visit, she answered 'none' to all of them.

Her friend explained that she needed to be more proactive – the role of marketing was to create awareness and, to an extent, what she had spent money on was doing that, but if not enough customers were coming to her, then she needed to put some effort into finding them. He also pointed out that, as she was a new business, no one knew about her, so they couldn't really be expected to find her; instead, it was up to her to make a difference and do some prospecting.

He helped her draw up a simple plan and told her that each day she should make 10 phone calls, send 10 emails, make 10 comments on social media and write 10 letters to potential customers. He explained that by putting in this sort of level of activity, in a week she would be reaching out to about 200 people and that, eventually, she would start to see results. It didn't matter if she did a bit more or a bit less, but she should aim to be consistent.

The purpose of all this activity was to get meetings with potential clients, where she would have the opportunity to showcase what she could do.

He suggested that after 2 or 3 months, she would work out which method worked the best and she could double the effort doing that, to further boost her productivity.

Leonora didn't want to do this, but she realised that she didn't have much choice so, even though it was a struggle, she persevered and every single day, she did her calls, letters, email and social media work. Gradually, as she got better, she started to make more appointments and get out to see more clients. After the first month, she had 2 sign-ups, by the second month she had another 6 and in the 3rd month she got 8. She also knew from her records that the telephoning and the letters had the biggest impact. As she got busier with work, she could reduce the amount of prospecting effort, but her friend had told her to keep doing it, even if it was at a reduced level, to ensure that she had a pipeline of customers for the future.

ABOUT THE AUTHOR

Born in Kingston Upon Thames, Janet grew up in Woking, Surrey and had a happy childhood featuring lots of swimming and ponies! After trying lots of different jobs, Janet started her formal sales career with Xerox Business Services, working in Croydon, Cambridge and London and selling outsourced document management solutions. She successfully worked in a variety of sales roles and developed expertise within the pharmaceutical, training, software and government sectors.

In 1996 Janet began work with Trans-Atlantic College, a small private college based in Dalston, East London. At the time, there were only a handful of students, but using her sales and business development experience, Janet helped to grow the college until, when it closed in 2012, there were over 650 full-time students and thousands of part-time students enrolling every year. Janet was Head of Business Development and was responsible for creating and recruiting a high performing sales and customer service team, ensuring that the College achieved and maintained appropriate accreditation. She headed up the Sales and Marketing Strategy and the HR function within the college and helped to deliver training on Interview Skills and Chartered Institute of Management modules on sales and management. This role involved travel overseas – one memorable contract included delivering training to 220 Nigerian government officials in one enormous training session.

Since founding Tadpole Training, Janet discovered a love for helping entrepreneurs and small business owners, many of whom have never sold before. Her wide knowledge means she can relate to the challenges faced by business owners on a day to day business and provide just the solutions they need to overcome their sales fears and concerns.

Academically, Janet has studied with the Chartered Institute of Management, MIT SLOAN, Massachusetts and is a Fellow of the Institute of Sales and Marketing Management and an accredited member of the Association of Professional Coaches, Trainers and Consultants.

Achievements

2016 Featured Business – Start Up of the Year 2015/2016, The Guardian newspaper

2016 Finalist – Sales Trainer of the Year, BESMA (organised by The Institute of Sales and Marketing Management)

2015 Winner – Start Up Business of the Year – awarded by Enterprise Enfield

2016 & 2015 Finalist – APCTC Trainer of the Year

2015 Janet became an accredited "Approved Adviser" with Enterprise Nation

2014 Janet was a judge at BESMA (organised by the Institute of Sales and Marketing Management) in the category of Telesales Professional of the Year.

An offer from Janet Efere

Dear reader,

First of all, thank you for reading this book and I hope you have found it useful and interesting. In many ways, this is just a condensed version of what I do every day – help small business owners and entrepreneurs sell more.

If you would be interested in finding out more about improving your sales skills and growing your business, then I would like to offer you a free gift. Come along to one of my workshops. I usually charge for this, but you can come ABSOLUTELY FREE.

All you need to do, is enter your details here and say you want <u>free entry to my next workshop</u>.

www.tadpoletraining.com/contact

I will send you a list of all the next workshop dates and you can choose the one you want to come on.

Not only will it be an opportunity to learn some really valuable sales skills that you can use straight away, I actively encourage participants to network with one another so you may even find new customers!

Whatever you decide, I wish you the very best of luck in your business journey and I really hope you enjoy prosperity and happiness.

Janet

Printed in Great Britain
by Amazon